Praise for *Love Does Not Win Elections*

Ayisha's book is essential reading for every rookie politician and for all those who want to see democracy thrive across the globe. Like others before her, Ayisha came to the conclusion that there was no point in just fulminating against the political establishment, whilst leaving them unchallenged even in her own back garden. It is clear from Ayisha's book that "more of the same will not get us anywhere". This book is an effective guide to new entrants to politics in many countries who do not have a powerful local sponsor behind them.

Atedo Peterside CON, Founder of Stanbic IBTC Bank & President of ANAP Foundation

In a highly revealing and witty narrative that exposes the intrigues, manipulations, corruption and hypocrisy that define the process leading to the nomination of candidates by the political parties in Nigeria, Ayisha Osori pulls no punches as she recounts how she sought a ticket for the House of Representatives on the platform of the Peoples Democratic Party and how it all unraveled. It is a compelling book for those who seek to understand the powers of political wheeler-dealers and the dangers they pose to democracy and good governance in Nigeria.

Olusegun Adeniyi, Author, *Against the Run of Play*

Nigeria has a lot of politics but hardly any economic development. The question is why? Ms. Osori's book does a fine job of answering this troubling question. This book is a baton. Those who are contemplating politics in Nigeria would do well to pick it up.

Feyi Fawehinmi

This was an enthralling read, and the author took me along all those dusty roads and airless rooms waiting for Big Man X or Big Woman Y. I gritted my teeth along with the author as we knelt before the aforesaid *Bigs* seeking political endorsement or favour. This book offers some hope and advice for how to change things.

Ayo Obe, Legal practitioner and former President of the Civil Liberties Organisation

Ayisha's gripping account reminds us of the depth of the work required to fix the Nigerian question at both ends of the spectrum – leadership and followership. This book exposes the pollution within the party delegate system and the minefield ahead for people who decide to upset an inglorious status quo.

Seun Onigbinde, Founder, BudgIT

Love Does Not Win Elections is a pitch perfect account of our primary process in Nigeria. If we weren't laughing we'd be crying as Ayisha courageously exposes the tragic process by which we nominate political candidates. This important work will inspire credible change makers, especially women, to lead the much-needed reforms.

Jacqueline Farris, DG, Shehu Musa Yar'Adua Foundation

Love Does Not Win Elections

LOVE DOES NOT WIN ELECTIONS

AYISHA OSORI

Published in Nigeria in 2017 by Narrative Landscape Press
1B Olatunde Ayoola Avenue, Obanikoro, Lagos State, Nigeria
+2347014522083, +2349090554406—7
contact@narrativelandscape.com
www.narrativelandscape.com
Second impression, 2018. Third impression, 2020. This fourth impression, 2024.

A catalogue record for this book is available from
the National Library of Nigeria.

Cover design by Adebayo Gbenga based on an original concept
by Shobola Ibukun
Layout Design by Shobola Ibukun
Cover Illustration by Black and Lee Creative Hub
Author's Photo: Chris Gloag

To my family and friends

"In nooks all over the earth sit men who are waiting, scarcely knowing in what way they are waiting, much less that they are waiting in vain. Occasionally the call that awakens – that accident which gives the "permission" to act – comes too late, when the best youth and strength for action has already been used up by sitting still; and many have found to their horror when they "leaped up" that their limbs had gone to sleep and their spirit had become too heavy. "Its too late", they said to themselves, having lost their faith in themselves and henceforth forever useless."
Frederick Nietzsche

"The credit belongs to the man who is actually in the arena, whose face is marred by dust and sweat and blood; who strives valiantly; who errs, who comes short again and again, because there is no effort without error and shortcoming; but who does actually strive to do the deeds; who knows great enthusiasms, the great devotions; who spends himself in a worthy cause; who at the best knows in the end the triumph of high achievement, and who at the worst, if he fails, at least fails while daring greatly, so that his place shall never be with those cold and timid souls who neither know victory nor defeat."
Theodore Roosevelt

CONTENTS

Chapter 1

Deciding To Run

I was new to party politics.

Why would I want to be one of three hundred and sixty members of Nigeria's House of Representatives, a club of the highest paid legislators in the world, notoriously ineffective and the subject of much public derision, who only have to sit for a minimum of one hundred and twenty one days a year? Why would I aspire to join this body's tiny contingent of women – seven percent at the last election – and subject myself to the bombast of so many Nigerian male VIPs who never get tired of hearing themselves talk?

Why would I even bother?

My friends joke that I have an aversion to ease and a built-in radar for suffering. One swears I have "punish me" tattooed on my forehead in invisible ink. When people were lining up before God to get their human dose of self-preservation, I was missing. This may have been a factor in my decision, but I had affirmative reasons for running as well.

It was late 2014, and Nigeria's two main parties were heading into primaries to select candidates for the general election which was due in February 2015 – it would later be postponed to March. I lived in Abuja, part of the Federal Capital Territory (FCT), which has two members in the House. One constituency includes the central area, known as the Abuja Municipality Council Area (AMAC) where I lived, and a nearby area called Bwari. The other includes the FCT's ever-growing outskirts: Abaji/Gwagwalada/Kuje/Kwali.

The single most important question a candidate must be able to answer is: "Why are you running?" I asked myself this question over and over as I made my decision, and wrote down my list of reasons for running, in no particular order.

I was tired of the dirty streets of Abuja. We had garbage piled up at every corner. On a windy day, the plastic bags strewn around surfed the air like kites. Sewage ran down the streets of some of the most expensive real estate in the country. The filth was driving me crazy, and posting pictures on Twitter was no longer enough. I knew that keeping the city clean was the duty of an executive agency, the Federal Capital Development Agency (FCDA), under the FCT minister. Unlike Nigeria's thirty-six states, a federal minister runs FCT, not an elected governor. But the National Assembly shared responsibility for approving the FCT Ministry's budget and passing laws for the FCT. Surely, as one of its representatives, I would have summoning powers and could crack the financial *koboko*?

I believed it was time to see more people who looked and sounded like me in politics. Since 2012, I had been the chief executive officer of the Nigerian Women's Trust Fund, a non-profit organisation focused on the increased representation of women in politics and decision-making. From that vantage point, I could see that the 2015 general elections were not looking good for women. We were going to remain far below the global target of thirty-five per cent female members in the legislature, and one reason was the small number of women running in the first place. In 2011, less than ten percent of candidates for the general election were women. By contesting, I would add to the numbers, gain first-hand experience of running for elective office, and become a more persuasive advocate for women's representation in politics and government.

The third reason was that I wanted women in government who knew and did better. I was ashamed of the response of women in elected office to the plight of the Chibok girls. They had been abducted by Boko Haram a few months earlier in April 2014 and symbolised all who had lost their lives or freedom to the insurgency while seeking education and a better life. After the abduction, our thirty-two women in the national assembly – twenty-five in the House of Representatives and seven in the Senate – split along party lines. The pro-government ones minimised the crisis; the pro-opposition ones made it a partisan issue. Many seemed not to care at all, including those in the executive.

Was it fair to focus on the few female legislators and let their male colleagues off the hook? Perhaps not. And yet, getting more girls into school has been a huge development issue for Nigeria, particularly in the northeast, which has abysmally low female literacy levels. You would think our female legislators would take special interest. If the twenty women in the United States Senate could write a bipartisan letter to President Obama urging action for the Chibok girls, then ours should have done more.

Over the last fifteen years, a few legislators have worked closely with civil society groups to pass bills to promote gender equality and improve the lives of women and girls, but many female legislators seem to have little interest in being associated with this cause. Activists routinely have to plead with them to get chairpersons for the legislative committees on women within the House and Senate. Instead of begging, we could be working to get unashamedly pro-women legislators into the national assembly.

Also, we do not know enough about how our government and political parties work. We have some ideas, we hear fantastic stories of influence and intrigue, but what is it really like? Is running for office really as wild a process as it seems? I was tired of not knowing, of hearing tales of the game of politics being dismissed as "beer parlour talk". We needed to demystify our politics. If nothing else, I would have my personal experience to validate or debunk the stories.

I thought the people of the FCT deserved more care; it was more than just home to the federal government. A naturally beautiful place with leafy green hills and massive rock formations, it is the fourth largest urban area in Nigeria after Lagos, Kano and Ibadan, with three million residents and growing fast. Many of the communities surrounding the power and affluence of the federal government have no motorable roads or running water. Some have no electricity, no industry, no commerce, little education and little motivation for being productive and engaged citizens. There was room to serve as an advocate, a voice for these communities and include them in the plans for the capital territory's economic and social progress.

Why not me?

I had been told, "You should run for office" enough times to make me think it was not such an unreasonable idea.

There is something about the typical Nigerian politician that makes one ask, "Surely we can do better?" Nigerians talk about politics all the time, around the dinner table or from behind keyboards. At some point, I thought, we should demand more of ourselves. Besides, how hard could it be?

Still, I worried how family and friends would react if I actually ran. Disaffection with politics runs deep; it has been a long time since it was viewed as a noble profession. "What is he looking for?" was the standard response in my parents' academic and public administration circles when they heard someone planned to contest elections. The indignation and befuddlement only increase when they perceive this individual as accomplished, and as such having better options. Educated? Check. Respectable job? Check. Considered intelligent, with a lot to offer the community? Check. Joins politics? Loser!

I had all those traits, and the more I thought about it, the more I thought these traits would make me a worthy candidate for office – not a loser. After all, I had a degree in law and two Masters degrees. I had practised law in a firm in New York City and returned home to work in the private sector for ten years; six of those in different roles in a multinational company. In 2008, I started writing weekly opinions about the state of governance and society and started thinking more deeply about the public sector. This led me back to Harvard in 2009 on a scholarship for my second Masters, this time to the Kennedy School to study public policy.

I moved to the Nigerian Women Trust Fund, a non-profit organisation focused on increasing the participation and representation of women in politics and decision-making in 2012 precisely because I wanted to be directly involved in public work. My professional experience meant I knew what it meant to be disciplined, deliver value to the bottom line, and be accountable to my managers and team.

Politics in Nigeria is not for the lily-livered. Not when you have also been socialised to be disdainful about those who get lured into it. I grew up with the narrative that success in the political process is designed for the worst of us, or maybe the worst character traits in all of us. Even leaving aside the history of violence, rigging and shameful behaviour, politics remained the field for those who had nothing better to do. This narrative accounted for a lot of the failures in Nigerian politics and government.

While mulling if I should run or not, I sought counsel from a few friends, including some who had actually dared to run for office. The votes were unanimous in favour of my contesting. Still, I was gripped with fear about the comments that would fly around as soon as my name came up in connection with elective politics. "What is she looking for?"

The narrative around women in politics in Nigeria is nasty and sexist. A common description for women who are involved in politics is "prostitute", and the stories about female politicians and campaigners being raped and verbally and physically abused were scary. This discouraged many women who by virtue of their expertise and experience could contribute to governance and improving the lives of Nigerians.

To my surprise, when they heard my plans, most were excited. Our lives were not improving at the pace befitting a country with so many talented and industrious citizens. Nigerians were beginning to make the link between the excesses of those in government, the insecurity and the poor state of social services. They were making the connection between the state of the country and the glaring incompetence of some who have had access to power and the steady decline in the quality of those who win elections. They saw that the space for political participation was closing. The disillusionment and complaints of Nigerians outweighed the promise of new ideas or faces. The state of Nigeria was unpleasant and untenable and many in my circles were beginning to question our beliefs about what our roles and responsibilities were with regards to politics and public policy. Perhaps we could not afford to stay out of the ring and go on simply watching with disgust.

As people cheered my decision, they also gave advice. I listened to them, and wrote another list for myself. No one had any illusions this would be an easy journey, or one without compromises. I needed my own compass: a guide to ensure that when I looked into the mirror I would not see a rodent, weasel, or someone I could not recognise.

I decided that I would abide by the rules of the game – except when it was impossible to; keep my opinions to myself (new one for me); visit, consult with, and seek support from people I would ordinarily want nothing to do with; wear my party's colours; and play it cool even when my intuition screamed I was about to be cheated.

On my "will not do" list was trade sex for access (yes, I was advised this could be an issue if I chose to run on a certain party's platform); eat my words; write obsequious articles about the then first lady, Dame Patience Jonathan; and wear aso-ebi with any person's face on it.

The advice and encouragement were the easy part. Later I would need financial contributions and boots on the ground to support my campaign. Still, the enthusiastic response was invaluable. It gave me comfort that I had made the right decision and that there were people who recognised that more of the same would not take us where we wanted to go.

Among my generation, the thinking that we had to get

involved in the public sector had become commonplace, reiterated every time two or more of us got together in the inevitable discussions about the state of Nigeria. But it was a touching affirmation from my parents' generation – those who had once enjoyed the best that Nigeria ever had to offer – to get their support. Later, they would tell me with pride how they ensured my campaign posters were all over their neighbourhoods. Some helped me in the quest to meet party leaders, some contributed to the campaign funds and others made introductions to anyone they knew could help – someone who might know someone.

They had raised us to be wary of politics, but they now recognised that the situation required more active involvement.

Chapter 2

Getting Started

The first thing I had to do was choose my political party.

There is not much to distinguish Nigeria's two main political parties: the People's Democratic Party (PDP) and the All Progressives Congress (APC), at least not in terms of ideology and core values.

The PDP had been in power at the federal level since 1999. The APC had formed, as a merger of various opposition parties, in order to wrest power from PDP, which it would succeed in doing with the election of President Muhammadu Buhari in 2015. When those parties held their merger talks, a group of people in civil society, including myself as the CEO of the Nigerian Women's Trust Fund, thought that we had an opportunity to help shape a new party as a kind of outside advisory group. We drafted provisions for the new party's constitution, which addressed some of the perennial issues that plagued other parties such as membership discipline, transparency with member registration, fairer primaries and affirmative action for women. But our high-minded efforts proved in vain. The APC constitution ended up being near identical to PDP's. Both parties are essentially vehicles to gain and keep power. Both are driven by factions and politicians who often wander freely from one party to another.

When friends and associates learned I was contesting the primaries under the PDP banner, you might have thought I had shaved off all my hair and was walking around naked; such were their reactions.

"You are committing political suicide by running under PDP!"

"You have killed your brand. Killed it!"

I did not even know I had a brand. I was amused by the melodrama, but the truth was that deciding what party platform to run from had caused me sleepless nights. In some ways, it was a weightier and more nausea-provoking process than deciding to contest in the first place. As a newspaper columnist, first with my column for *Thisday*, *The Lawyer*, and later for *Leadership*, and as a public commentator on radio and television, I had been scathing about the PDP's politics, policies, attitude to governance, and the detrimental impact of years of PDP rule on the practice of democracy and the development of Nigeria and Nigerians. We still lived with less than 4500 megawatts of power after years of PDP-led initiatives costing billions of dollars, the government had lost the monopoly over violence resulting in terrorist groups operating in the Niger Delta and North East; insecurity was the order of our lives and years of under-investment in education and health had lowered the quality of life for everyone.

Yet, the party reveled in arrogant statements like "PDP will rule for sixty years" and "There is no vacancy in Aso Rock," the presidential palace. They smacked of a total disregard for the people, vindicating the nagging suspicion that our votes did not count.

So, PDP was not a natural choice. However, APC was not the automatic choice either. I knew a member of civil society, much older, who planned to contest for the same AMAC/Bwari seat. He had started preparing early, and joined APC ages ago. I did not want to struggle for the same ticket with him but a few friends convinced me that my sense of propriety did not matter. I went to the APC national headquarters on Blantyre Crescent in Wuse 2, a district of Abuja, to register as a member. Accompanied by someone who knew his way around, I met the officer responsible for registration, who promptly instructed me to come back later. There was some story about forms not being available and registration of members being closed for processing – consultants were handling the registration to ensure all party members had proper identification cards. When I went back a few days later to follow up, I left without making any progress.

A few evenings after, I found myself at a sit-out for Bring Back Our Girls, the spontaneous civic movement that had sprung up after the Chibok abductions. These sit-outs were held at the centre of town, at the Unity Fountain in Abuja's Central Business District and many people stopped by on their way home from work or other errands. On that night, I sat next to Pastor Toyin Matthews, who planned to contest for the FCT's sole Senate seat and shared my plans and experience. She took me to Habib Gajo, the ward chairman of PDP for Wuse district which was my ward. Gajo was sole custodian of the ward members' register and responsible for registration and issuance of membership cards. He was a stark contrast to the typical party ward chairman: fluent in English and Hausa, educated and anointed with the gift of the gab.

Seventeen thousand naira lighter, I had my PDP card. I hadn't chosen the party; the party chose me. Of course, the process was not finished. It would take nearly three times that initial amount to get my party card regularised with the right signatures to validate my backdated membership. According to the rules, you had to have been a registered member of the PDP for at least two years before you were eligible to contest. The big bound ledger, which was the Wuse Ward members' register, had strategic gaps in the entries, empty lines across the years, which were waiting to be filled in retroactively with the right names.

In a sense, by joining PDP, I had ended up following the advice of the organisation that I led. At the Nigerian Women Trust Fund, we advised aspiring female politicians to be strategic about their choice of party and the position they aimed for. For instance, there was no point contesting for the Senate from a district where a governor concluding his second and final term in office had indicated interest in retiring into the Senate. Likewise, and despite some exceptions, it was hard to win a legislative seat if you were not in the same party with the state governor. In the FCT, that meant your best chance was with the incumbent party at the federal level, which was still the PDP. All in all, PDP was the better bet for the seat I was interested in.

In any case, there was no going back, especially after I paid for and picked up my expression of interest and nomination forms at the PDP office on 22 October 2014. A few people pleaded that they would refund my expenses and get me the APC forms instead. It made no difference. I often advised female aspirants to be unemotional about their choice of party because our political parties were not about ideology or ethos but cash, expediency, malleability and influence. It was time to follow my own advice. When circumstances shoved me towards the PDP and I made my decision, I was at peace with the choice. Not everyone in PDP could be bad, the same way not everyone in APC was good. Those who want change and strive to make a difference cannot afford the luxury of all belonging to one party.

I had talked to many people, but I still had to talk to my mother. I looked forward to telling her that I was contemplating elective politics with as much enthusiasm as a cat looks forward to a soak. I was sure her version of "what is she looking for" would be scathing and include something about fairy tales and head in the clouds. My mother retired from the Central Bank of Nigeria and had left a strong record of service through her years at Ahmadu Bello University, Zaria; Usman Danfodio University, Sokoto, and as the first female registrar of a federal university, at the University of Technology, Minna. It was unthinkable that I would buy the forms before talking about it with her. When I brought it up, she was casual. As if I was only asking her yet again to look after my sons while I travelled for work. She seemed fine with the general idea.

I filled in the details about what party platform I was running on (this provoked a mild exclamation), who I had seen and what I had to do next. I needed one million naira from my personal funds, which she managed, so I could pay for the party forms I needed to become a candidate.

My mum has a clear philosophy of money: Don't spend it. How to save it: don't spend it. How to grow it safely: In treasury bills, and don't spend it.

She refused my request. Instead of giving me a million naira from my funds, she would loan me the money interest free, repayable whenever. Now I could buy my forms, but I still had no money for the campaign apart from my salary. It was clear that I would not have access to my savings. This meant I would have to do something I found unpleasant and I was not skilled at – asking for money. I had always been frugal myself. Growing up, perhaps my allowance was generous, or maybe I had few needs – in hindsight, probably a mix of both. It was not until my second year at the University of Lagos that I realised that the ever-expanding wardrobes of my friends was not the result of parents with great style, but rather of self-sponsored trips to Tejuoso Market.

"Where do you get the money to buy new things so often?" I asked my friends.

"What do you do with your pocket money?" they replied.

Now my savings were off limits, and I had no trust fund and no fairy godmother or godfather to subsidise my electoral adventure. I prepared an estimated budget of expenses. It gave me a basis for asking. I could say, "This is how much I need" and it would let me know how well I was doing and when I could end the fundraising campaign.

The budget covered the cost of nomination and expression of interest forms, as well as other fees and charges. There were the substantive expenses of campaigning: staff, materials and logistics. There were also the many meetings I would need to hold with party delegates and various people in the field. Gifts were expected, and the norm. They could not be avoided.

I listed the budget items: visits with delegates; meetings with party leaders, officers and influencers; campaign posters; consultation gifts; transportation (hiring cars, trucks, drivers); campaign team salaries; media; communication (phone calls and SMS messages); contributions to party wards and associations; and specialist advisory services (tax consultants and campaign experts). My final estimate was fifteen million, two hundred and fifty three thousand and two hundred and fifty naira.

Next, I made a list of those I could ask to support my campaign that was a mix of: people who had said in the past "You should run" or "It is people like you we need in government", those who were wealthy and financially secure and generally supportive of me and those who I knew cared about politics and governance and would be happy to contribute.

I sent out emails with the subject line: "Time for Business Unusual". It was an expression that Amina Salihu, the co-chairperson for the Nigerian Women Trust Fund, liked to use. I attached a picture of me collecting my nomination and expression of interest forms from the FCT PDP chairman, a copy of my resume and a two-page letter explaining in more detail why I was running.

Some money had already come in, even before I sent out the request. On 24 October, I got my first donation for one hundred thousand naira. I was so thrilled, and immediately called to thank the friend who so thoughtfully sent it to me without my even asking. From then until 5 December, a day before the primaries, I raised a total of nine million four hundred and seventy one thousand naira. I even got a final donation after it was all over, from a kind colleague who believed in the goal of increasing women's political participation.

The contributions ranged from one thousand to two million five hundred thousand naira. Many asked to remain anonymous, but I cannot forget the names and faces of each of my twenty-six donors, nor the effort and untold costs of many like my mum, sister, family friends, aunties and uncles who came around constantly to pick up campaign posters.

The fundraising process was not all pleasant. I miscalculated with some of my acquaintances, placing a strain on our relationship. There is nothing more annoying than minding your own business and then being put in the position of having to say no, or being forced through the indignity of ignoring calls and emails. I felt bad even at the time for putting them in that situation.

Yet for all my innate discomfort with asking for money, I found campaign fundraising to be a positive, even powerful experience. More than just show me that I could overcome my aversions, it proved to me that there are Nigerians ready to match their words with action and ready to give to a cause or person they believe in. The joy that some donors expressed at the fact that "one of us" was finally sticking out her neck and getting into politics bordered on glee. Their enthusiasm motivated me. It surpassed the power that doubt, my constant companion, had over me.

Some days, the donations came in steadily; during other periods, a whole week would go by with nothing coming in and a major expense looming. That would trigger a wave of letters and emails requesting for donations for my campaign.

As the day for the primaries loomed, I got bolder, put

aside my middle-class feelings of shame and self-sufficiency and practically harassed a few friends to contribute. It was inconceivable to me that they would not support the campaign financially. This gave me another perspective into the common theory that "Nigerian politicians have no shame". Ambition, greed, need, hunger and desire will always trump shame, especially in a permissive society.

I needed other people's money, and I spent a lot of my own as well. My savings may have been off limits but my current account certainly wasn't. In hindsight, the ease with which I dipped into it again and again is worrying.

Money is the lifeblood of our political process. This was a critical lesson for me to learn first-hand. A group of female politicians had once insisted to me that their number one challenge to accessing power through the ballot was "lack of funds". My response was: "So if you have no cash, will you not run?" Now, I understood. My naivety must have shone through, like poorly cooked moi-moi in a transparent plastic bag.

There is no contesting primaries and general elections without money. I should be made to write out this line nine million four hundred and seventy one thousand times – that's how much, in naira, I raised in contributions in a period of two and a half months.

I spent every bit of that and more on seven cost centres.

The first was the salaries and logistic support for the campaign team and helpers. The second was the formal cost of contesting – the assorted payments the party required in order to formalise my status as an aspirant.

Third came networking expenses. It was essential to make friends and build alliances across the party and with influential people. I had records of at least five hundred and seventy two thousand two hundred and ninety naira in this rubric, but suspect I spent quite a bit more. I had taken people gifts and taken some out for meals, bought them recharge cards, given them money for breakfast, lunch or dinner, depending on the time of day when we met and even covered pizza for their children.

The fourth cost centre was branding: posters, business cards, customised letterhead and fees for defacing structures with my campaign posters. I lost count of how many people collected posters and funds to post them. I was certain that all this had cost more than the half a million naira I could account for.

The fifth category included miscellaneous costs such as communication (phones, sim cards and airtime), photocopies, affidavits and assorted banking charges.

The sixth category was transport. Here, I spent far less than was apparently the norm. Early on, someone had drawn up a budget for me that allocated twenty million naira to campaign cars. I did have to request for a jeep from the car rental service because of the state of the roads in some parts my constituency, and this cost a little more than a saloon car. Besides, I often drove myself, in my own car, and never tracked how much fuel I was buying.

The seventh cost centre was by far the largest: engaging the delegates. By my accounting, I spent five million eight hundred and fifty six thousand and seven hundred naira on this process. It included the meetings with delegates and ward chairmen; the gifts of rice, fabric, and sewing money we distributed on ward visits; hosting the female delegates for lunch; and of course, the almighty delegate dues.

Aspirants and contestants need funds to pay for party forms and hidden administrative charges, and to pay for the usual tools of a campaign: posters, stickers, media coverage, among others. A candidate also needs money for every politically related discussion with party members, delegates and constituents. Every rally, gathering of delegates, visit to an influencer's hut, house or palace, costs money. So does every small meeting, even with the campaign team. This is because our prevailing social and political etiquette requires that the person who instigates a meeting should provide.

A candidate is expected to provide for transportation of the participants, their refreshment and whatever else is considered adequate incentive for the audience to receive the message. Civil society organisations and donor agencies practice this too. It is impossible to run without money.

In an Al-Jazeera documentary covering Nollywood actor Kate Henshaw's bid in 2014 for the PDP ticket to represent Calabar Municipal/Odukpani constituency Cross River State in the House of Representatives, she says of the process "It all ends with money." It was true. But thanks to the contributions from friends, family, and other supporters who valued what I was trying to do, the money also expressed belief and confidence in me.

My funds went a bit further because I got a discount. The PDP waived nomination form fees for female candidates, so my total in assorted charges came to two million naira less than male aspirants had to pay. I felt like a hypocrite, because theoretically I was against waiving fees for women. In too many stories I had heard, this concession ended up working against female candidates, who were sometimes ordered by their parties to give way to male rivals precisely because they did not pay the full amount. This could happen even when the woman was the more popular candidate. It was as if a woman's ambitions and aspirations are only as valid as the naira she paid. In one state in the North Central zone, a female aspirant reported that a party that waived a hundred per cent of the fees for women turned round and restricted women to contesting only for seats in the state legislature "because they were not paying for the forms." It seemed absurd, but it reflected how high-minded party policies, which look good from the outside, clash with the actual apparatus that run the party. Reportedly, APC and PDP together made nearly four billion naira from selling forms to aspirants. Those with the power to spend these funds probably felt aggrieved by the thought of women not adding to the purse.

Waiving some or all of the fees for women does make it easier for more women to make the decision to contest, and that ability to participate is important. It provides experience for the aspirants and options and diversity for the people and the party. I would have paid anyway, but my engagement with delegates, ward chairmen and party leaders would have been two million naira poorer for it. I still have mixed feelings about the waiver of fees for women even after being a beneficiary of the policy. It is a Greek gift. The way it operates in practice in Nigeria's political parties, seems to reinforce the idea that women are participants of lesser value – that the ways in which we contribute to the party count for less, and that men can shut us out at any time.

The waiver left me still needing to pay five hundred thousand naira for the expression of interest form, fifty thousand naira to the PDP North Central Zonal office, and three hundred thousand naira to the FCT PDP secretariat as part of the process. The last one was off the books. It was not on any list of payments I had seen and I had not budgeted for it. I later heard that some other aspirants for the AMAC/Bwari ticket had collected and submitted their forms at the PDP national office in order to escape paying this arbitrary fee. They found the local party officials waiting for them later on and had to eventually pay up to proceed.

I had stalled at first before collecting my forms on the advice that I should secure the support of various influential figures before I committed myself to running. It was fortunate that I thought better of this, and did not wait until just before the deadline. It turned out that it would take more than a week to get my forms ready for submission. I needed signed nominations from thirty registered party members, tax clearance certificates, and copies of my primary and secondary school certificates. I had never seen my primary school certificate and was not even aware that schools issued them. I tried to find out if certificates for higher degrees such as university would suffice. It turned out that having a Ph.D. would mean nothing for this purpose. Apparently, people get doctorate degrees without going through primary and secondary school.

I had help from Zuby, a veteran of many political

campaigns and my first campaign team member. Recommended to me by Hajiya Ireti, he was a wiry, small man, who could have been in his sixties, spoke little English, and knew the workings of the PDP machinery in the FCT inside and out. It was to him that I handed my nomination form so he could get me the thirty signatures. Each person had to include his or her name, party identification number, voter registration number and signature. I was so glad when the form returned in one piece I pretended not to notice that all thirty entries were filled in the same handwriting.

As the primary election season revved up, the news each day featured photo-ops of politicians picking up or handing in their forms at the political party offices, and a few friends thought I should submit my forms with a bit of fanfare: news cameras, band of supporters and a small press conference. I thought better of it. It might be good to get some publicity, but deep down I thought the noise was premature.

On 31 October, I triple-checked my forms, made copies like any good lawyer, and asked Zuby to meet me to turn them in. I did not feel up to matching the energy of the usual inhabitants of the party office: the praise singers and assorted supporters for hire, with their forced smiles and open palms. Instead, I parked two streets away and had Zuby come find me. I explained how the documents were arranged to follow the flow of the forms, and he walked off. I distracted myself from hunger by editing a report. Within ten minutes Zuby was back. Apparently, I was required to provide a checklist of the documents I was submitting. I made two – one for them and one for our complete set of copies, which I wanted officially acknowledged for my records.

An hour passed before Zuby flashed my phone. When I called back the legal adviser was on the line. She informed me that my application was not yet complete for the following reasons: Both sides of my permanent voter's card needed to be copied, my membership card did not indicate dues paid, and I needed receipts attached to it, because everyone else would have receipts, and my secondary school WAEC results were a mere notification of result as opposed to the actual certificate.

I tried again to advocate for my university certificates. She was quick to set me straight. She had been part of this screening exercise several times before, and no one cared about higher degrees, just primary and secondary school. I thanked her and confirmed that I would do just as she asked and submit my forms when I had all the accompanying documents.

I called Gajo, my ward chairman, and went to meet him. I wanted to sort out the issue of receipts for membership dues. These were not the types of surprises I liked. We drove to the home of Hajiya Ireti. She was a long-time Abuja politician who had run for office several times unsuccessfully (though popular belief held she had actually won the highest number of votes in the 2003 Senate race in which she was declared the runner-up). She was generous with advice to female candidates and a darling of civil society advocates for increased women's political participation. On the way, Gajo railed about the legal adviser not knowing anything. Apparently, in the past, women did not have to pay dues. Besides, what party ever gave receipts for dues and contributions?

As he got out of the car, Gajo's parting advice was: "Submit your documents with Hajiya Ireti, and you will see, they will not ask all these questions."

I took his advice and once I got a copy of my secondary school certificate results, I handed the forms to Zuby to submit along with Hajiya Ireti's. I had to let my team and patrons play their part.

Chapter 3

Patrons And Networks

I soon learned that the paperwork meant little without the right backers to pass it along. This was true, it became clear, of the entire project of running for office. I needed to line up my patrons and I was advised to start from the top. In party politics, the proverb that holds that the biggest masquerade comes out last did not apply. If the big masquerade came out first, it would clear the field for a candidate.

The game changer, I was informed, was Ahmed Muazu, at the time the national chairman of PDP. He was a high-level dignitary in the pecking order of Nigerian big men: a former chairman of the National Pension Commission, former two-term governor of Bauchi State, with a long list of chairmanships and directorships on his resume. When he was made party chairman, he had an open file with the Economic and Financial Crimes Commission (EFCC), for allegedly looting nearly twenty billion naira from Bauchi State. Be that as it may, he was the political rainmaker, the deal clincher, and if I could get his support for my candidacy, the ticket was mine.

No one seemed willing to take me to see him, though. "Stop asking me to help you see Muazu, I am not going to take you to him," an older friend said in exasperation when I had asked for the third time. Some people had advised me that I would be foolish to commit almost one million naira for the PDP candidacy forms if I could not see Muazu and get his support. But if I waited for his support, I would miss the filing deadlines. While I worked on meeting Muazu, I decided to find alternative support from other big party men and women.

I started with the biggest masquerades I had access to: former ministers and former chairmen of the PDP. Uncle Bello was a friend of the family, who had been close to my late father, so I did not need an appointment to see him, just confirmation that he was home. Humble pie tasted like wet newspaper. I had not visited in years. I was not a fan, and had named Uncle Bello a few years earlier in an article I had written about always-ready-to-serve government men, the ones who had taken part in every federal administration since I was in secondary school with little positive development to show for all their work. I numbed my discomfort about seeking his support by reasoning that those who ask for directions do not get lost.

We were alone in his living room. I sat on the floor in front of him, with my legs tucked underneath me and my feet to my right in supplicant's pose. He welcomed my visit but raised some issues. The issue of indigene status – having parentage that rooted me in the FCT, which I did not – might be an issue, he said. Besides, the party leadership and the president, Goodluck Jonathan, apparently wanted the incumbents in the FCT, not fresh faces. I told Uncle Bello I would continue to take people's advice and would appreciate whatever help he could give. He promised to introduce me to some party leaders, but was not encouraging. "Do not waste your money," he said as I took my leave.

Next, I met with a former minister, Alhaji Liman, whose portfolio once included the FCT. Mallam Hassan took me to Alhaji Liman's house one evening to share the news that I was considering contesting on the PDP platform. I came to know them both from being members of one of the many online discussion forums set up by Nigerians to discuss Nigeria. Both were in their fifties, thick around the middle, well educated, sophisticated, with years spent in government and experience politicking. Mallam Hassan could open most doors: and who opens doors in politics is everything, in more ways than one.

As we drove across town, I was pleasantly surprised that a former minister did not live in Maitama or Wuse 2 districts, where most power players roost. We turned off a main road in Garki into a quiet tree-shrouded lane. The gates were flung open for us. As we walked from our cars, Mallam Hassan steered me away from the main house towards a one-story building to the right.

The doors opened up to a reveal a large court-like room with a generous space of plush carpet guarded by leather sofas lined around three walls. As we chatted and waited for Alhaji Liman to join us, a young man came in to offer us drinks.

Alhaji Liman was tickled that I wanted to contest elections. But why not in Kogi State, he asked? I said that I had briefly considered Kogi, my state of origin where my parents came from, but since I had never lived there and hardly visited, I did not think I had any grounding to contest there. Abuja had been home since 1996, and my entire immediate family of siblings and mother lived in Abuja too. Alhaji Liman promised to consult with a few people about whether running in Kogi or FCT would be best for me. It turned out that Kogi was a no go area. Through him, I spoke with a brother of the governor of Kogi, who advised, "As a lady, FCT is better for you." Kogi politics was notoriously violent and base.

Alhaji Liman put me in the care of Amir, one of his assistants, telling him to introduce me to the various FCT party leaders. It took a few weeks to pin Amir down, but he was useful. Through him, I got a better sense of the cast of characters in the party's FCT production. One was the chairman of the PDP Chapter. I first thought his name was Wai Wai Suleiman, until I realised that Y.Y. were his initials. We went to visit him.

On the drive there, Amir asked me what I had for the chairman. I had nothing. "*La la la*, you cannot see people like this and not have anything for them. I have one thousand dollars. I will give him and then you can pay me back in naira." He fished out a roll of dollars and showed it to me. My heart started racing. I did not want to work out what percentage of my salary this was.

"I cannot give him one thousand dollars! What for?" I asked. Even to myself, I sounded like a balloon being squeezed in the middle.

"See, my sister, you might not have to give him anything again, but by giving him this one thousand dollars on your first meeting, *za ki burge shi*. Every time you call him, every time you want to see him, you will have access."

Y.Y. Suleiman's office was in Garki Area 4, in a two-storey building originally intended to be a home. After Amir introduced me and told him who I was from, Y.Y. said, "You are a powerful woman. I have already been told about you."

I smiled encouragingly. Amir gave me a look suggesting he was re-evaluating his opinion of me.

"Dr. Bello Mohammed told me about your interest in contesting a while back. We spoke on the phone?" Y.Y. asked, plodding through my blank gaze. I had no recollection of such a call, but I went along with it. "Yes," I smiled. "Uncle Bello spoke highly of you and said you would provide good counsel."

Like all good politicians, Y.Y. took a phone call while we were establishing our connections, and moved to the balcony attached to his office. Amir whispered that this was the best time to present my gift. I stretched out my hand to receive the money but Amir ignored it. He joined Y.Y. on the balcony, and after a few minutes of talking and laughing they came back into the office. Y.Y. thanked me. On the basis of the two introductions, I was his sister and he would do all he could to support me.

My next target was Dr Ahmadu Ali, who had served as PDP chairman between 2005 and 2007. His daughter Maryam was my friend. We met one evening after work and drove to his office in Maitama.

Dr Ali asked me a few questions about the AMAC/ Bwari wards and area councils. I had all the answers to Maryam's surprise. Dr Ali dismissed as nonsense the idea that FCT belonged to indigenes. He promptly made an appointment for me with someone he said it was important to see – Ambassador Ayuba Ngbako.

I promised myself before the meeting with Dr Ali that if he was discouraging I would give up on the idea. Now I gave myself permission to continue. A lead to consult with someone else was positive, and I had other party influencers to see.

Muazu remained the big prize. Amir and I agreed that whenever Muazu was in the office he would let me know. I called frequently to check since I never got any calls from him to that effect. One evening just before 8p.m., as I was finishing up for the day, I called Amir, as part of my routine. They say be careful what you ask for. It was one of those days when I wanted nothing more than to go home and stretch out my legs. But Muazu was in the office. Amir told me to come over immediately.

Amir met me outside to help me past the throng at the gate. The entire complex of the PDP National Office was buzzing as if it was the middle of the day. We went straight to the second floor, past the guards, and stood in the corridor leading to Muazu's office for about thirty minutes before Alhaji Liman came out. In that time, I watched a stream of people walking in and out of the inner sanctum – some recognisable, others expecting to be recognised. When Alhaji Liman spotted me, he was visibly surprised. He ushered me in through the door that could only be entered on invitation, and wanted to walk with me straight into the chairman's office until two security aides objected. Alhaji Liman went in himself and then came out and said I should wait in another room, where until a few minutes ago the deputy senate president had allegedly been waiting for over an hour.

I crossed my fingers and went through my opening lines. I knew I would not have much time with Muazu, and would be competing with swirling distractions and demands. After ten minutes, Alhaji Liman came back to say it was best we try again on Monday. The chairman was very tired; he was still in a meeting, he had not prayed and wanted to go home.

"Besides," Alhaji Liman continued, "Bala Mohammed is really the main person to see."

Bala Mohammed was the FCT Minister. I told Alhaji Liman I had not had any luck with seeing him. Alhaji Liman said he would work something out, and I should expect to hear from him.

Two weeks later, it was mid-November, the primaries were nearing, and I was still trying to see Bala Mohammed or Muazu, when an unexpected opportunity to see Muazu presented itself.

The Federal Ministry of Women Affairs and Social

Development invited me, in my capacity as CEO of the Nigerian Women Trust Fund, to join the advocacy team being supported by UNDP's Democratic Governance for Development (DGD) project. The team's brief was to meet with key figures regarding support for women's political participation during the elections. Among these were the party chairmen.

Frankly, I found these meetings with the political parties on gender inclusivity fairly useless, but it was one of the few things the donors were interested in funding, and so we all played along. For one, even though the woman leaders of the various parties were invited, I had not been to one meeting where the team brought a list of female candidates with the positions and constituencies they were contesting, in order to productively engage the party leaders. We never extracted anything but vague promises. In one meeting, the national chairman of a party told us squarely, "It is not time for women yet."

This time, Muazu had confirmed his availability to meet with the team. We had landed the big fish. I was sceptical. I had been to enough of these meetings where the chairman confirmed participation but sent the party's national woman leader to represent him. Moreover, the meeting had been scheduled at exactly the time when my campaign team wanted me to meet Bwari delegates at a hotel in their area.

"Are you sure he will be there?" I asked Mufuliat, the DGD representative. Once I was convinced, I made a few phone calls and rescheduled my campaign meeting to later that afternoon.

Eight of us were ushered into Muazu's office in Wadata Plaza in Wuse Zone 4. As we settled around the conference table, Muazu asked twice if this was the UNDP meeting on his schedule. Mufuliat and Iran Ajufo, the Director of Women Affairs at the Ministry took time to explain that it was and stated our mission. Slowly, other members of his team, including Mrs Kema Chikwe, the national woman leader for PDP filed in. Focused on the piece of paper in front of her, Ajufo read her speech completely oblivious to Muazu's frequent glances at his watch.

Finally, it was time for introductions and my turn to speak came.

"Chairman, good afternoon," I said. My name is Ayisha Osori and I am the CEO of the Nigerian Women Trust Fund. At the Fund, we are worried that despite Mr President's good intentions towards women in decision-making, as evidenced by the number of women on the Federal Executive Council, the on-going discussions and negotiations around automatic seats will ensure that women are left out of the equation." Legislators wanted to keep their seats, and governors at the end of their second term, wanted seats in the Senate as well as the power to determine their successors.

"That's your opinion," Muazu retorted almost before the last syllable left my lips. "Maybe you have been talking to APC." It was such an unexpected response that a few of us burst into laughter.

Introductions out of the way, Muazu started his response with the typical rhetoric of male politicians around the world when discussing women's roles, by enumerating the women in his life. "I have sisters, three wives and six daughters," he announced. My daughters are closer to me than they are to their mothers. They tell me first when they have boyfriends." It followed, according to Muazu, that no one loved and respected women more than he did. These protestations of love from men in authority do not translate into wanting to make the world a better and safer place for all women. They fail to realise that their power and wealth provide limited protection for their female relations who still have to navigate and live in a world that is still to a great extent dismissive and disrespectful of women.

We listened to Muazu, even when he said things that were not true. "PDP forms are free for women," he claimed. Mrs Chikwe could have corrected him, but maybe she herself did not know, since she was not contesting.

"So what can we do if women are not coming forward to contest?" Muazu concluded.

"No, I do not agree sir," Sharon Ikeazor, a member of the advocacy team responded. She was a former national woman leader for one of the parties that folded into the APC. "Women are coming out, sir. Here is one of us, Ayisha. She is running under your party for the House of Representatives."

He looked interested.

"What constituency?" he asked.

"AMAC/Bwari," I replied.

At this point, Mrs Chikwe, who had been quiet, unfurled sharply like a flag shooting up a pole on a windy day. "This is not the place for this," she said loudly.

I turned to look at her in surprise along with most of the others in the office.

"You need to go round and know all of us first," she continued.

No one responded to her, but Muazu had lost interest and moved on.

After the meeting, I made my way to the front where people were taking pictures and then when I could, told Muazu that it was important for primaries to be held in Abuja. I kicked myself afterward for forgetting to add that if primaries did not hold, PDP would lose the elections to APC.

"Who said primaries will not hold?" he asked

I was learning that rumours were an integral part of the primary election process, playing a pivotal role in how the political industry and government runs in Nigeria.

"Primaries are not going to hold."

"PDP is not going to announce the results of the primaries on the day of the primaries. The ballots will be taken away and only the national headquarters will announce winners."

Sometimes stakeholders surreptitiously fly kites and there was no way to substantiate a story until it did or did not happen.

There was no harm in confirming.

"That is what we keep hearing sir," I replied.

"It is not true."

"Okay, that is good news. I'll leave something on your desk along with my card. I look forward to your support."

I had taken advice to turn an article I had written about the possible repercussions of the PDP's decision not to hold primaries on the election results into a letter to President Jonathan and copied Muazu as chairman of the party. I dropped a copy of the letter on his desk and left the room to those who needed evidence of the meeting for reports.

I felt encouraged by the short interaction with Muazu and resolved to try to see him again, preferably with someone he knew well. I learnt from my mum that a family friend, Uncle Isa, was close to Muazu and immediately called him to ask if I could visit.

It was the first time in twenty years that I was visiting Uncle Isa at home. I usually saw him at functions or family events. The last time I visited him at his home he was still managing director of Jos Steel Rolling Mills. Then he lived in a sprawling mansion. Now he lived in a flat that looked like it was still being completed. My heart hurt. Visiting him gave another perspective to working in government and being honest. If he had made the most of his position, he would be living in much grander settings. How do we reconcile the opulence that government officials are entitled to with the fact that they have no decent pensions and that government is unable to honour its own part of the contract to look after the welfare of everyone, including those who have served the public? Whatever money most people have earned and saved is spent on expensive private education for their children, private health care, generating power and providing some semblance of security.

Uncle Isa confirmed that he was close to Muazu and had access to him. He was also clear that whatever influence he might have was because he never asked for favours for himself.

"It won't be hard to see Muazu," he said. "The problem is whether he will have time for a quality conversation. He always has lots of people around, it is almost impossible to see him in private."

Did I know that!

I assured him that I understood. I knew that sometimes the mood was not right to bring up certain issues and told him that he did not have to raise my aspiration if the setting was not right for that topic.

While I was there, he called Muazu's principal secretary, who said he was at a wedding and would call later. Uncle promised to schedule a meeting with Muazu and take me along. I did not hear from him and failed to follow up. When I remembered that I had opened up this line of communication, it was too late. I never got to meet Muazu again, and even if I had, it would have made no difference to the outcome of the primaries.

"Have you tried the First Lady?"

"Have you asked the First Lady for her support?"

"Has the First Lady endorsed you?"

From the moment I floated the possibility of running for office, people began asking me these questions. Dame Patience Jonathan, the wife of President Jonathan, had campaigned furiously in 2011 for more women in decision-making as part of her Women for Change Initiative. In the run up to the 2015 elections though, she was quiet except for a few causes: her husband, Nyesom Wike (Minister of Education), Emeka Ihedioha (Deputy Speaker) and Uche Ekwunife, a female member of the House. Wike and Ihedioha were contesting for the PDP gubernatorial tickets for Rivers and Imo respectively, while Ekwunife wanted to advance to the Senate.

Why wasn't I looking for Dame Jonathan's support as well? No one suggested I see Mrs Bala Mohammed who played the de facto role of first lady in the FCT.

Why this obsession with the First Lady? As it happened, this was a topic that had weighed on my mind for several years, in part because of my experience managing the Nigerian Women's Trust Fund and my curiosity about the real obstacles to women successfully contesting for office.

I was trying to understand the role of first ladies, not just in promoting women's political participation and representation, but in governance and society in general. First ladies all over the world used their husband's presidency to influence and shape policy and promote projects around issues they care about (Sarah Brown for education advocacy and Betty Ford for equal rights for women) to varying degrees of success and acceptability by the public.

Some Nigerian first ladies have been credited with advancing the cause of women in Nigeria, and quietly, and not so quietly, influencing appointments on the national and state level. This slowly solidified first ladies as a practical route to negotiating for the dividends of power for women, some of which include the Women's Commission in 1989, the Ministry of Women Affairs and Social Development in 1995, state laws on gender and equal opportunities in Ekiti and increased numbers of women leading local governments across some states. There were also the women-focused pet projects of first ladies that on rare occasions outlived their reign.

The strength of the family connections of women who were winning elections was also something worthy of exploring. For instance, of the twenty-six women who have been elected into the Senate since 1999 (some more than once), forty-six per cent have been daughters or wives of presidents, senate leaders, former military and civilian governors, a former secretary to the federal government and a former senate president. This category of female senators not only constituted the majority in the Fourth, Fifth and Seventh National Assemblies, they also had the higher rate of re-election. In the United States of America, widow succession initially played a huge role in increasing the number of women in Congress. Up until the 1970s, a large number of the women who entered the Senate and the House of Representatives were elected or appointed to succeed a late husband, or on rare occasions, a late father.

Dame Jonathan's appeal in 2011 when she zigzagged the country campaigning for increased women's political participation and inclusion was for the minimum thirty-five per cent representation of women recommended by Nigeria's 2006 National Gender Policy. The gender policy was based on the 1995 Beijing Platform for Action's call for thirty per cent of national legislative seats to be held by women because it was considered the minimum critical mass for women's representation to be impactful and at this time, the representation of women in the national assembly was seven per cent.

When the votes were tallied after the elections on 9 April 2011, there were fewer women elected into the national assembly when compared with the number elected in 2007. The numbers in the Senate dropped from nine to eight and from twenty-seven to twenty-five in the House of Representatives.

Without the benefit of knowing which women won their elections due to the influence of the First Lady, it is hard to assess the efficacy of Dame Jonathan and the Women for Change Initiative in advocating for increased women's participation. A sample of the winners of the

2011 general elections from the national assembly would indicate that what some winners had in common was not the support of Dame Jonathan, but the strength of their individual connections to male authority figures.

Men also benefit from ancestry within Nigeria's political industry. Indeed, amongst those responsible for deciding who serves Nigeria, nepotism remains as strong an ideology today as it was in 1966 when it was listed as one of the reasons for the coup of 15 January. Using family ties and blood relationships as a basis for granting access to power and privilege has been vital to the military's hold over Nigeria. In his book *My Watch*, President Obasanjo admitted to using this tactic when he arranged for the children of politicians in the First Republic to work with him in 1999. This has become an effective way to keep the elite quiet and complicit in the continued exploitation of Nigeria.

The key differences between the men and women whose access to power might be questioned is that male public officers, by virtue of patriarchy are conferred automatic legitimacy and do not have the burden of expectations to improve the lot of men or light a candle for other men. Women struggling for more seats at the table are scrutinized more carefully and held to higher standards. This is why assessing how effectively and differently they wield power and influence is important.

The belief that I could get the PDP ticket through the "very powerful" First Lady, Dame Jonathan, was so strong amongst politicians and some of the people I consulted with that I would have been a goat not to try. It was of course entirely up to me to get to her, as the advice never came with an offer to visit the presidential villa.

"How do I get to the First Lady?"

No one in my immediate circle had any links and as I explored options, I was advised to write some positive articles about her. That way I could get invited to see her, or at least improve my name recognition with her camp. I gave this some consideration and I even opened a blank page on my laptop once, to make a list of things I could possibly write about her; but I could not think of anything to say besides how absolutely entertaining she was.

Eventually I got a number for a fixer who could get me to Dame Jonathan. Our first attempt consisted of a few hours spent one Saturday going through the names of those who had the ear of the First Lady. I knew none of them. We narrowed down to Brandy, a woman with easy access to Dame Jonathan and spent a considerable length of time discussing what type of whiskey I could arrange for the first visit to Brandy. All I had to do was whip out two hundred and fifty thousand naira which I did not have. After a few follow-up calls, the fixer stopped calling.

Another approach was to follow up on a "try Bola Shagaya" lead. Mrs Shagaya, a wealthy businesswoman, was a skilled survivor of regime changes and had a permanent pass to Aso Rock regardless of who the temporary tenants were. Mrs Shagaya and Dame Jonathan were so close they often appeared in public wearing identical outfits.

As I searched for a way in, I noticed a defect: my network was not primed for politics. I knew who to call for the latest academic paper or data on early marriage or another witty response to *Why Women Can't Have It All.* I had at least half a dozen people who could explain the issues on gas supply for electricity. But I did not know a single person who knew Mrs Shagaya well enough to take me to her.

I found out where she lived from someone who had no intention of taking me to see her and decided I would wear down her security barriers with perseverance. At least once a day for a few weeks, on my way to work or back, I drove by her house and asked if she was home and if I could see her. I left a letter on the first day introducing myself and sharing my dreams and why I was the type of candidate she (and the First Lady) should support. Each time I went back, I left my business card and tried to win over the guards by giving them generous tips. I hoped they were not just tossing my cards into the flowerbeds. One morning I insisted that the guard take the card in while I waited. He returned with another gentleman. I wound down the car window as he got within ear range.

"Good morning. Thanks for coming out to meet me," I called out.

"Good morning, Madam." He looked down at my card, then at me. "How can I assist you?"

I explained that I wanted to see Mrs Shagaya and mentioned that I had dropped off a letter a few days ago.

"Are you from a bank?" he asked almost before I finished.

"No, I am not," I said slowly, as I gestured towards the card he was holding. "I run a non-profit and have explained in the letter why I would like to see her."

"Do you have a copy of the letter here?"

I did not. "I can drop off a copy for you or email it," I said. "Whatever works best? Bring a copy? What is your name?" I whipped out my phone. "That way I can address the envelope to you," I explained.

"Do you know anyone who knows her?" He was already stepping away. "Because that is the best way to see Madam; come with someone that she knows. But to just see you like that," he kissed his teeth, "it would be hard."

I thanked him and drove away.

Sharing my difficulties getting to Mrs Shagaya with an associate, I learned that I might be able to get a connection through Senator Khairat Gwadabe. Senator Gwadabe was elected in 1999 on the PDP platform to represent FCT in the Senate but did not secure the PDP ticket for the 2003 elections. Tall and regal, Gwadabe, a lawyer, was a member of Ilorin's Abdulrazaq family – famous for producing the first lawyer from the North. She was married to Lawan Gwadabe, who was military governor of Niger State from 1987 to 1992.

We met at her office in Asokoro late one afternoon. After we settled into a three-seat sofa opposite her desk, I introduced myself and explained why and how I was in the race for the AMAC/Bwari ticket. I needed her support reaching Mrs Shagaya or Dame Jonathan. She said she could only offer advice.

"I will not dissuade you from running but it is unlikely that there will be primaries in PDP," she said. "The incumbents will all keep their seats while aspirants will be urged to step down."

The dynamics around politics in the FCT had changed since her time in office. Now, it was more difficult for non-indigenes to win. One reason was the track record of Hon. Nicholas Ukachukwu, who represented AMAC/Bwari in the House of Representatives from 1999 to 2003. The story was typical of public officers in Nigeria – serve yourself in office, and use that money to remain in power, ascending from position to position. After serving as Chairman House Committee on the Federal Capital Territory and Chairman of the House Committee, Oil and Gas, he was now a perennial gubernatorial candidate in Anambra State. His time in the FCT was not remembered fondly.

Senator Gwadabe felt there was one possible way to cut through the party support for the incumbents – the gender angle. But this meant my primary audience would have to change. Instead of the PDP leadership and the FCT minister, I should look to the First Lady and president. Senator Gwadabe thought Chief Felicia Sanni and the Minister of Women Affairs could help in gaining access and amplifying the message.

We spent a little time framing messages that might resonate with these four people. With Chief Sanni, I would acknowledge the role she had played over the years in getting people elected. I would laud Hajiya Maina's reputation as a persuasive political operative and the message for Dame Jonathan would be that she could crown her work with the Women for Change Initiative by working to increase the number of women in the national assembly. I would urge President Jonathan to improve his record-setting appointment of the most women ever in the federal cabinet, and encourage him to ride the applause into the electoral arena, bolstering Nigeria's reputation in so doing.

Senator Gwadabe was upset that the Nigerian Women Trust Fund had never invited her to any of our programmes. She was the first female senator from the North, and one of only three women who made the senate class of 1999-2003. She lost her bid to return to the Senate when she did not win the PDP primaries for the 2003 election and moved to ANPP where she campaigned hard but lost the battle to get Hajiya Ireti elected into the Senate. She sounded like a formidable politician, and I felt inadequate for not having her on the Fund's radar. I told her that I agreed that we were myopic in focusing only on serving legislators, who, barring a handful, did not have time for us. It was definitely a strategy worth considering to engage former female legislators in our advocacy. I promised to rectify our omission. She advised me not to bother reaching out to her.

I followed up the conversation with Senator Gwadabe by reaching out to the Federal Minister of Women Affairs and Social Development, Hajiya Zainab Maina. She had a reputation for being an effective and astute grassroots politician. She sat on the advisory board of the Nigerian Women Trust Fund and our relationship was professional. I had not been smart enough to invest in politically strategic relationships by visiting people in positions of authority on a regular basis, accumulating credit for the day I would need something. As minister, Hajiya Zainab was not an obstacle to our work, and she was honest about how the Fund was perceived by the First Lady's milieu. It was a hear-no-evil, do-no-evil relationship.

As chief executive officer of the Fund, I expected to be asked to resign from my position in order to seek political office. But the Board was practical: win the primaries first, they instructed, then we will accept your resignation. For now, this was an adventure to gain experience for the team. Whatever the case, I needed to tell the minister before she heard the news from anyone else.

Hajiya Zainab was generous. She told me what a good person I was, but complained that I stayed away, like a stranger. I promised to do better. She said she was glad that more young women were joining her generation in the arena so they could retire and know that there were others to carry on. She confirmed that I should really see the FCT minister and Ahmed Muazu, but she was non-committal about making that happen. Neither she nor I mentioned the First Lady. We exchanged numbers and she told me to let her know if there was any way she could help.

As I continued to work on a connection to Mrs Shagaya, I hit upon two other options for getting to Dame Jonathan.

Ms Onyeka Onwenu, the famous musician who was

the director general of the National Centre for Women Development and Chief Felicia Sanni, the president-general of the Market Women's Association.

Chief, who was over seventy years old and a retired banker, was a formidable mobiliser and a fixture within Dame Jonathan's campaign entourage. She was popular with civil society organisations that needed to reach grassroots women with ease.

One day, I got a call from Yusuf, one of my peers in the Eisenhower Fellowship who heard I was contesting and wanted to find out how the process was going. Dame Jonathan came up. I confessed to getting nowhere with plans to secure her support. He offered to introduce me to Chief Sanni saying that she and the First Lady were close. He was certain Chief would help me if he asked. "She calls me her son."

As soon as Yusuf sent me her number I called her and introduced myself as her daughter – Yusuf's sister. She was pleasant and made it easy to keep calling. Every time I called she was on her way out of Abuja or still somewhere else. One morning in early November I tried again on my way to work and she was home. That day the Nigerian Women's Trust Fund was hosting a meeting at the Chelsea Hotel with male politicians who were, as usual, late. As we waited the obligatory hour and a half extra for our guests to arrive, I decided not to waste the opportunity, jumped into a jeep at the car hire park and dashed across town to Utako. Even on workdays most locations in Abuja are easy to get to. I could be there and back within an hour.

The number of slippers outside the front door prepared me to meet the curious gazes as I pushed in and entered the room. I dropped to my knees to greet Chief and the other women, and told her who I was. She asked me to take a seat to her right. The women sat in a row on a sofa to her left while she sat behind a table, like Piers Morgan interviewing a panel of guests. On the mantle were pictures of Chief Sanni with President Jonathan.

The conversation continued while I put my phone on silent and relaxed into the chair. Suddenly she asked her guests if they wanted any wine, and without waiting for them to answer, jumped out of her chair and asked me to follow her. I followed thinking she needed help bringing out the bottles and wondering if it wasn't too early to drink.

Once we entered her bedroom, she told me to sit so we could talk in private and gestured at the ubiquitous white plastic party chair. Being Nigerian, I had a strong appreciation for the power of begging. I knelt before her to begin my elevator pitch. "Get up, get up," she urged.

But I remained on my knees while I repeated what I told her over the phone: "I want to run for the AMAC/

Bwari seat in the House of Representatives and I want you to support me."

She asked me a few questions.

"How long have you lived in Abuja?"

"Since 1996."

"Do you attend ward meetings?"

"Yes, I do. I met Jummai there at the last one." I mentioned the name of the lady I had the fortune of bumping into outside Chief's house as I walked through the gates. She had offered her services as a campaigner at that ward meeting.

Chief snapped her head up like it was pulled back with invisible string. "Don't give her shishi. You hear me? Don't give anyone shishi," she said, eyes gleaming.

I nodded. She asked me to get up and sit.

"People do not know that the main reason I started mobilising women was for politics." She showed me pictures of the women she mobilised for the Transformation Agenda for Nigeria (TAN) rallies. TAN was a non-profit organisation that had raised hundreds of millions of naira to "create jobs to sustain families and spread the gospel of President Goodluck's transformation agenda through visible empowerment of the people and educate voters with a view to discouraging money politics and electoral malpractice".

In preparation for the mega TAN rally, Chief said she had gone to Sapele to place orders with a company that specialised in carving anything out of wood. They made round poster boards, which looked a little like oversized hand held fans, painted them white with car paint and branded them with messages in support of re-electing President Jonathan. She brought them home to hide until the day before the final TAN rally in Abuja. She and her women were a hit. After the rally, a minister called her and gave her twenty million naira in appreciation. She said she spent a little under one million for the entire operation. I was impressed. Chief made sure her jolly public persona did little to reveal what a shrewd businesswoman she was.

When the subject returned to me, I was pleased when she confirmed that Jisalo, the incumbent who I hoped to unseat, was widely disliked. She asked me how the PDP congresses to select delegates went and I admitted that I was not even a delegate. "Give me a day to find out what is going on and come back to see me on Wednesday," she said as she walked me to the door.

It took another week and a half, two more visits with fabric and cartons of juice, and several phone calls before I sat with her again. She asked me to meet her at home one morning; there were people she wanted me to meet. Her living room was packed with women wearing aso ebi.

She asked someone to bring in an extra chair. The only available space was at the back of the room between the sofa and the window adjacent to the front door. So when she introduced me, asking me to stand up, everyone had to turn in their seats to see me. Next thing I know, Chief pledged my contribution to the Market Women's Association for their support for my aspiration. When the meeting was over, she whispered to me to "bring like twenty thousand." I dashed to the nearest ATM, breathing a sigh of relief that it worked, and went back to her house. They had moved outside the gates of the compound, which was at the end of a close, and were sitting in a circle with refreshments. Chief was sharing campaign stories. I sat on the chair she pointed at next to her, and tried to follow the conversation. There was one about a woman who thought Chief was her mate – one small girl who was married to a governor and thought she was better than everyone and how she eventually put her in her place. She mimicked the woman. We all roared with laughter. Every few lines she would pause to marvel at the generosity and care of Dame Jonathan, and how well the entourage was fed. "The woman wan use food kill us," she repeated.

As other women shared their own stories, I handed over the pledged money. Chief asked how the campaign was going. I gave her a quick summary: who I had seen, who had been helpful, and the doors I still needed opened. She told me Dame Jonathan had decided not to support or endorse any individual aspirant because she was supporting all women and no woman in particular. After a few minutes she asked me to call Y.Y., the FCT PDP chairman. When he picked up the call, we greeted and I asked him to hold on for Chief Felicia Sanni. She hailed him, teased him and then mock-threatened him if he did not deliver her pikin as the FCT's first female member in the House of Representatives.

A few days later, Maryam and I stopped to see Ms Onyeka Onwenu at her office at the National Centre for Women Development. I was over an hour late for the appointment with her and was tempted to call and reschedule. The danger that she would conclude that I was not serious was real.

The first time I called to let Ms Onwenu know I was going to contest the primaries and would like her support, she told me off. First, for ignoring all her invitations to events with the First Lady. Second, for communicating board related matters with her by email instead of with letters or phone calls. There was no defence and I simply pleaded for her forgiveness.

"I do not appreciate being used," she went on. "Obviously, you have my numbers, why are you only just calling me now that you want something?" She sounded as if she was simultaneously doing something unpleasant, like scraping something disgusting from the bottom of her shoe.

I said I had no excuses and she hung up.

I followed up the call with a few text messages, first apologising again and then keeping her updated on my milestones. The last time we had spoken, I felt the frost thawing, and I didn't want to lose the window of goodwill.

Luckily for me, she was still at work and we did not have to wait long to see her.

She was very welcoming and had nice things to say about Maryam's dad when I introduced her as Dr Ali's daughter. I wasted no time in going to the root of our visit. I was there to follow up on my letter requesting for her assistance in securing the support of Dame Jonathan for my bid to represent the AMAC/Bwari constituency.

Ms Onwenu confirmed what Chief Sanni had told me. Those close to Dame Jonathan had agreed that no women would be taken to the First Lady for her support or endorsement. The plan was to support the aspirations of all women.

Into the ensuing silence, she asked, "Who have you seen within the party? Muazu? Secondus?"

"I have not seen any of them but I have been trying and I have not given up. Can you help? I would really appreciate it."

"Okay," she said. "I can commit to doing that for you because I have a good relationship with the PDP leadership. But you have to play a part. You let me know whenever Muazu is in the office and then we can meet there and I'll barge in with you. I can do that for you."

She had another question. "Do you know Mrs Kramer?"

"No, I don't."

"You don't?" Her voice went up. "You should. This is a woman that makes things happen." She picked up her phone.

I was intrigued and looked at Maryam who was nodding her head in confirmation.

She leaned over and whispered, "She used to be my dad's secretary when he was chairman."

We listened to Ms Onwenu tell Mrs Kramer about me and which party ticket I was seeking. Soon it became clear that Mrs Kramer already had a candidate for that position. I wondered if it was the incumbent.

"You did not start early enough," Ms Onwenu told me as she put her phone down. "People have pitched their tents. Anyway, you do your part, let me know when Muazu is in his office and I will get you to see him."

I thanked her for her time and said I had brought her

something small, some ankara fabric, which I knew she wore, but she refused to take it. I explained that over the last couple of weeks, consulting and advocating for support for my aspiration, I had learnt that I had to leave something behind – money, fabric, a befitting gift.

"Bad practice," she responded. "We should not encourage it."

I knew what she meant. I had been privy to some of the gifts other aspirants were leaving behind when they went seeking the support of party leaders: expensive watches, bundles of dollars, and hours of use on private jets – things that most people, women included, could not afford. If we could not beat them even when we joined them, then we should be working to change the practice.

Ms Onwenu was my last lead to Dame Jonathan, but I was not particularly saddened by my failure to meet the reluctant patron saint of female politicians. My view was that the power of first ladies – at least the way that most of them used it – lacked legitimacy. Like a blunt knife forcefully used, they were likely to do more harm than good in the long run.

Chapter 4

I Am Not An Indigene, So What?

When I decided to contest for a seat from the FCT, and not Kogi State or anywhere else, I had two considerations in mind. First, I believed in Nigerians taking root and contributing to the community wherever they lived or worked. Second, there were precedents in the FCT, where people who were not considered indigenes had been elected to represent the territory at the national assembly.

Admittedly, the precedents were old and had not been renewed in the last few elections. But it was only when various PDP chiefs told me the president and the party were committed to keeping FCT for the indigenes that I realised how strong the underlying tensions were between various ethnic groups who called FCT home.

I followed up on Dr Ali's advice to consult with Ambassador Ngbako, an indigene of the FCT, and after a few phone calls, I met with him on 23 October at his office on a quiet hidden close off Aminu Kano Crescent. Ngbako was the first FCT PDP chairman. He had served Nigeria as ambassador to Gambia, and was a director in one of the many government agencies no one was aware existed.

He was small, dark, blunt and loquacious.

"Don't count on the support of the Gbagyis."

He said the Gbagyis had been generous and had no apologies for insisting on self-representation. In 1999, Khairat Gwadabe, who was not an indigene, won a seat in the Senate, and an Igbo man represented AMAC/Bwari in the House of Representatives. That House member used the position to advance himself, and had since gone back to his state to make a series of unsuccessful bids for the governorship. Gbagyis were indigenous to Niger, Kaduna, Nassarawa and Kogi, but the only place that they had was the FCT. Zephaniah Jisalo, the incumbent in the seat I sought, was Gbagyi.

Dark, stocky with a trademark wide grin, there had been no meteoric rise for Jisalo. He plodded up the political food chain most notably as an employee of that bastion of election management, the Independent National Electoral Commission. He chaired Abuja Municipality Area Council (AMAC) from 2004 to 2010 and joined the House of Representatives in 2011 representing AMAC/Bwari constituency.

New contestants were not welcome, Ngbako said. He informed me that a few days earlier, at a meeting in his house, the elders of FCT took two decisions: that the incumbents would be returned with Jisalo in the House and Philip Aduda in the Senate, and Peter Yohanna, the chairman of Bwari Area Council, also an indigene, would not contest the House of Representatives seat for AMAC/Bwari.

Yohanna who was in his late twenties or early thirties (accounting for the "small boy" moniker) was considered by the PDP establishment to be the most serious challenger to Jisalo's incumbency.

"Instead of starting the wrong way, don't start at all," Ngbako said. "You will look like you are taking a gamble or being an opportunist, and that will reflect badly, especially if the outcome is not favourable.

"Now that you are here, you can still be useful," he added, with a wide smile that showed off evenly sized and arranged teeth. "Take a message to those whose ears you have access to: FCT indigenes want to be able to nominate ministers. Since 1999, FCT has not had an indigenous minister representing them on the federal executive council, not even as the minister of the FCT."

The indigenes of FCT were adopting the practice common in other states and considered political positions within the FCT their exclusive birth right. There was advocacy to amend the Constitution to give the FCT the status of a state, which would include Abuja in the famous "federal character" provision. The Constitution's Section 147 demands that the president appoint at least one minister from each of the thirty-six states, "who shall be an indigene of such state".

I did not realise how much this state of things coloured the calculations of those involved in the FCT political industry. If the FCT minister wanted peace and the support of the Gbagyi landlords, he knew to fill political appointments with the sons and daughters of the soil. Both elective and appointive positions in the FCT were becoming the reserve of indigenes alone.

One evening in early November, after my meeting with Ngbako, I met up with someone who laid out some of the intricacies that would allegedly drive the outcome of the primaries and elections.

Isiaka was introduced to me not long after I made the decision to contest the primaries, as someone who would provide insight into local politics and help with my campaign. I did not find out until much later when I mentioned to Hajiya Saudatu who introduced us, that it was near impossible to pin him down for a discussion, that he was conflicted because he worked for Peter Yohanna.

I stopped calling until he made contact and asked to meet at City Park in Wuse 2, behind Diamond Bank. He had information for me.

Religion was going to be a factor in the AMAC/Bwari primaries. Until recently, there was a loose understanding of "rice and beans" in the emergence of candidates and winners in FCT elections – one Muslim, one Christian. Now all three current elected officials in the national assembly were Christian indigenes (the Area Councils were still serving the required menu). And the senator, Philip Aduda was openly playing the religious card by appealing to the leadership of the Christian Association of Nigeria (CAN) to intervene with President Jonathan to save his seat.

Divisions within FCT went even deeper. Among the Gbagyi, the people of Bwari felt like perpetual bridesmaids, critical to winning elections but themselves never elected. No one from Bwari had been selected for a major appointment such as ambassador nor to represent the AMAC/Bwari constituency in the House of Representatives. It was always AMAC, never Bwari. In addition, within Bwari, no one from the minority Hausa ethnic group had ever been elected to chair the area council. The 2015 elections were a chance to set things right. If Yohanna could ride the popular support of his people up, into the House of Representatives, then his deputy, Matawalle, a member of the ethnic minority in Bwari, would serve out the remainder of the term as area council chairman and create a new precedent.

The personalities of the incumbents in the national

assembly, particularly Aduda and Jisalo, strengthened the sentiments for change. They were unpopular in Bwari for being arrogant, stingy and disrespectful. In the primaries for the 2011 elections, the majority of Bwari delegates voted for Yahaya GwaGwa and Jisalo had not forgotten this. It took him over two years after his election to visit Bwari in his official capacity and he allegedly never missed an opportunity to hurl invectives at the people.

In addition to fuelling religion as a factor in FCT politics, Aduda had succeeded in alienating the party and the FCT minister. As pay back, the minister was allegedly sponsoring Jibril Wowo's bid to return to the Senate. Wowo had won the election to the Senate in 2007 as a member of the All Nigeria People's Party (ANPP), but his election had been annulled by a tribunal, along with that of Nasir Mohammed who won the AMAC/Bwari House seat. The grounds for annulment were that some candidates of other political parties had been unlawfully excluded from contesting. After the tribunal's decision was upheld on appeal, by-elections were held and Philip Aduda and Adamu Sidi Ali, both of PDP, won the seats to the House and Senate respectively. Voters had little interest – only eleven per cent took part in the Senate vote and six per cent in the House elections. There were the usual complaints of ballot box stuffing and voter intimidation by the ruling party.

Wowo had since made his way into PDP and had been the Senior Special Assistant to the FCT minister on political, budget and national assembly matters until he resigned and picked up his nomination and expression of interest forms.

This was the background to a meeting hosted by President Jonathan on 31 October, where PDP officials for the FCT were instructed to protect Aduda's seat. As a result, FCT minister, Bala Mohammed held a meeting at his house the following Sunday with Y.Y. Suleiman, Peter Yohanna and Jibril Wowo amongst those in attendance. Those with aspirations were told to stand down; the party had taken a decision to return the incumbents. None of the female aspirants were invited to that meeting.

I had received several calls asking me what happened at the meeting but now, through Isiaka I learnt for the first time what was discussed.

Yohanna declined to step down, saying he had to discuss with his people, who put him forward for the position. According to Isiaka, Yohanna was confident that he could win the primaries if they were held. Plans were underway to file a petition with PDP to forestall any decision not to hold primaries. The leadership of the party needed to know that PDP would lose to APC if they fielded Jisalo. The people of Bwari would rather the party lost than give their votes to Jisalo.

However, there was a chance that Yohanna would be persuaded not to contest and Isiaka wanted an Option B because he had control over the delegates. The selection of the Bwari delegates had been designed to deliver two things: Yohanna's win in the primaries and a member of the minority community taking over from him to become chairman of Bwari Area Council.

Amongst other stakeholders, the best scenario to manage all the permutations around personalities, ethnicity and religion was for Hajiya Ireti to emerge as the candidate for the Senate and Yohanna for the House. This would provide the same end results and take into consideration seniority and dues paid.

Further education on the indigene-settler issue in FCT came unexpectedly during a visit to a non-indigene delegate, Charles. He was convinced the primaries were going to be settled over one issue – the stake of indigenes and non-indigenes.

Charles had moved to the FCT in 1981, when Abuja was being built. He was an engineer and project manager supervising the construction of the city. Thirty-three years later, neither he nor his children could get a job in the

Federal Capital Development Authority, the entity through which the FCT minister executed his responsibilities, even though Charles's children, all raised and educated in Abuja, were qualified engineers and lawyers. According to him, at that time, not one of the twenty-eight political positions in the FCDA was held by a non-indigene.

Some of the beneficiaries of indigene politics in the FCT could barely write their names when they became chairpersons of area councils. Some who had made it to the national assembly were not qualified for most professional organisations. But they could become politicians: provisions in the Constitution such as Sections 65(2)(a) and 131(d) provide that office-holders need not have more than a secondary school leaving certificate. Political parties interpret this to mean only a secondary school leaving certificate is valid for eligibility. The problem with this provision is two-fold. One, it meant our politicians, charged with making law and policy and implementing development plans, had limited education and exposure. It meant that while our politicians were not qualified to work in the private sector – with the discipline and knowledge that this would require, they could work in government. Two, it sent a clear message in a country of low literacy rates and matching low investment in education, research and development that education was not important. If you could aspire to the highest offices in the land without being well educated, then education was of little consequence.

The major decision to have the capital of Nigeria at the geographical centre of the country was reportedly to blur historical ethnic divisions. The FCT was meant to be a neutral place, where the country could start over, do things right and build unity around our diversity. Instead, Abuja and its people had absorbed the toxins that the politicians, some of whom had held office since the seventies, brought with them to the new capital. Since 1976, only one person south of the River Niger had been minister of the FCT – Mobolaji Ajose Adeogun. In my area council, AMAC, there had been some chairmen and administrators who would be considered southerners, but only up to 1999. Since then, all four chairpersons elected to lead AMAC had been indigenes of the FCT. It was not for lack of trying.

On the evening of Monday, 17 November, Isiaka called me to tell me that Yohanna had agreed with the party that he would not contest the primaries for the House. Apparently, a discussion with EFCC had helped him come to this decision.

The Bwari delegates were mine for the taking.

Chapter 5

Being An Aspirant

One evening, as a friend visiting from Lagos and I settled down to dinner, I got almost simultaneous calls from Gajo, my ward chairman, and Zuby. They both asked if I could meet up at Hajiya Ireti's house for matters related to the campaign. Zuby said it was a good time to get the details of Hajiya's membership and voter registration card for my nomination forms. Gajo called to finalise my ward recommendation letter.

There was only one answer, and so I invited Toni along for an after-dinner adventure. He had been the very first person to donate to my campaign, and called regularly to find out how I was doing. I knew he would get a kick out of the trip.

There were lots of people at Hajiya Ireti's place when we got there. The front room and two side rooms were full. Hajiya and a group of young people were in one of them. After I exchanged pleasantries with them, Hajiya and I walked out together so I could get her details to complete the forms and introduce her to Toni, the author of several books.

Zuby, Gajo, and Umar Farouk were in another room. As soon as I walked in, Umar Farouk said loudly, "I hope you have the three hundred thousand naira for your letter."

"What three hundred thousand naira?" I asked turning to Gajo.

"*Gaskiya* the letter must be accompanied with your contribution to the party," he replied. "Otherwise you will face stiff opposition at the ward meeting. You are unknown, so members can raise objections to a letter commending you."

A letter from my ward attesting to my good standing with the party was one of the aspirant-screening requirements. Zuby and Salisu, one of his friends, told me to let them handle negotiations on my behalf. I went out and chatted with Toni and Hajiya Ireti. Every couple of minutes, Zuby would come out to caucus with me and then have a side bar with Salisu. Then they would go back into the room with Farouk and Gajo. I offered the full amount requested if they would throw in a delegate seat for me. After an hour of back and forth, I begged Hajiya Ireti to intercede and we got the amount reduced to half of what they asked for, with nothing promised or counter-offered for the delegate seat.

I did not have that kind of cash on me. I had to drive back home with Zuby to pick up what I had and head to an ATM to get the balance. It was past 10p.m., and Toni, who had an early flight back to Lagos, begged off the rest of the adventure.

I handed over the money to Zuby and drove him back to Hajiya's with the agreement that he would get the letter from Gajo the next day and bring it to me. I returned home feeling satisfied.

A few days before the deadline for the submission of forms, I got a phone call shortly before midnight, as I was preparing to shut down my laptop and go to bed. It was Mallam Hassan. He asked me to meet him at the home of a former speaker in Apo. There were some important people he wanted to introduce me to.

"This is a test," my brain flashed in the nanosecond before I said, "Okay," in the most neutral voice I could muster.

He asked if I knew the house.

No.

Did I know the area?

No.

He gave me directions. I paid almost no attention, so consumed was I with the thought of getting dressed and driving across town from Maitama to Apo in the middle of the night.

"Got it?" Mallam Hassan asked.

"Yes, thanks. See you shortly."

I hung up and contacted a trusted confidant and asked if he thought it was okay to go. "Go," he answered. "You have no idea who will be there and how useful they might be." I sent a text message asking Mallam Hassan to send me directions by text, changed and jumped in my car with my laptop.

Whatever this meeting was, I was prepared to wait for hours without squirming. I had learned the hard way that the only way to wait gracefully is to have something to do while you wait. In Apo, the streetlights were off and the shopping mall that was to serve as my landmark was completely enveloped in darkness. Somewhat apprehensively, I wound my window down and asked the men at a police checkpoint for the mall.

When I got to my destination I was immediately led into a dining room where Mallam Hassan and two men sat. One was an ex-minister, and the other, was a certain Sir Shuaib, who I had never heard of but was clearly supposed to. It is futile to be honest in these scenarios so I pretended I had, and sat down at the table with them.

Hassan gave me a generous introduction: my work with the Women's Trust Fund, my membership of intellectual platforms, and my writing for *Leadership* and *Thisday* newspapers. "Now, she has decided to join you in the trenches and is running for the House," he said. "She needs your support and guidance."

When he finished, he turned to me and said, "I am handing you over to Sir Shuaib. He is one person I know who can push through anything. He is a bulldozer."

I thanked Mallam Hassan and said I looked forward to Sir Shuaib's support and guidance. Sir Shuaib asked me two questions.

"How close are you to Ahmed Muazu?"

"I don't know him sir."

"How well do you know Bala Mohammed?"

Before I could give the same answer, Mallam Hassan cut in. "Zero."

"This makes things harder," Sir Shuaib said. He instructed me to call him the next day.

I was at the ex-speaker's house for less than thirty minutes.

I never saw the bulldozer again and only spoke to him one other time after at least a dozen calls and text messages. He picked up that one time to tell me to call him back later.

Late night meetings are one of the most often-cited

challenges to women's political participation in Nigeria. In my twelve weeks as an aspirant, I was only invited to this one, and was under no obligation to attend. I chose to go and the meeting was not helpful. Yet it could have been; I might have found Bala Mohammed and Ahmed Muazu there, and in a singular moment of lucidity they could have decided to break the party's pro-incumbents policy and say, why not? Let's have a young (by Nigerian standards) female member of the House for the FCT, and see what damage she can do to the status quo. Either way, if I had not honoured the invitation, I would never know.

If there were a husband to say no to my leaving home after midnight for that meeting with Mallam Hassan and his friends, words might have ensued, or at the very least a three-day dose of the silent treatment. Maybe that's where the challenge lies – navigating and balancing marital expectations.

When I scan the couples I know working across private, public and development sectors, I wager that the majority of men in this scenario would forbid their wives from attending a midnight meeting, out of concern for safety and respectability. One would offer to drive his wife there and sit in the car until the meeting was over. One or two would demand to be part of the meeting.

Yemi, an aspirant for the PDP ticket to represent her

constituency in the House of Representatives was dynamic, confident, and articulate about the issues and solutions. She had a supportive spouse who was also from the same constituency and often accompanied her for meetings with party and community leaders. They both had political pedigree, which in Nigeria means little more than having a recognisable name from an established or emerging political dynasty. Yemi's husband would often speak, sharing his thoughts on why his wife was the best candidate. Yemi said she could not count the number of times people at these meetings would ask her husband, "Why are you not the one running?"

When I worked in a law firm in New York City between the late 1990s and early 2000s, there were times lawyers needed to pull all-nighters or near all-nighters, but these were not the norm. It is probably easier for spouses to handle a call from the office informing them that it is going to be one of those nights, than it is to accept a call after midnight and a spouse jumping out of bed and into a car. There are certain professions, among them investment banking, medicine, security where late nights are part of the job. Does this constitute an obstacle to women being successful in these professions? Why is politics different?

For women in politics, the late-night meetings are a challenge on multiple levels. There are security concerns.

Despite police checkpoints, it is never safe to be out late at night. It increases the risk of exposure to armed robbers and carjackers, and for women in Abuja, there is the Abuja Environmental Protection Board to contend with. The AEPB considers it one of their duties to pick up women at all hours of the day, whether walking along the street, standing in front of their houses or public places or even sitting inside cars, on suspicion of being prostitutes and forcefully rehabilitating them at a cost to government of five million naira for every fifty women "rehabilitated".

There are also concerns about sexual abuse and promiscuity. Presumably women worry more about the former while men fret about the latter. There is a narrative in Nigeria that only women of easy virtue are interested in contesting elections or participating in party politics. This narrative is as pervasive as empty water sachets at a motor park. It makes it less likely that female politicians will report being raped or molested, and more likely that husbands will forbid wives from participating in politics. The narrative favours those who enjoy the status quo. Female politicians have reported demands for sex from party leaders in exchange for electoral success, but no one has ever been prosecuted.

Women who have worked hard and built a career do not want to be associated with promiscuity, for their sense of self and for their families. And although rape, sexual harassment and consensual sex can, and often do take place during the day, there is a sense that for many, the risks or possibilities of these happening are higher at night.

Part of the problem is the culture of late-night meetings amongst politicians and how prevalent and popular these meetings are in the first place. They cannot be practically banned; sometimes there are exigencies that make meeting at night necessary or hard to avoid. Whether the meetings are efficient and effective is another issue. I have been to a few meetings with politicians that started during the day, but I could tell would go on way into the night. The meetings did not start on time, and once they did, there was so much effusive camaraderie in the room that it was hard to keep the participants focused on the agenda. Add the deep love politicians have for their own voices, and efficient meetings are out of the question. If you are not present, you might miss something important. However, there is no guarantee that being at the meeting will result in an attendee having any actual input in decisions. There are stories of politicians meeting from 10p.m. to 2a.m. with no decisions taken. When the meeting officially ends, many, including women scurry home. Then the remaining men make the decisions in the car park as their drivers listen in.

Spouse's support and concerns for security aside, where

female politicians have young children, there is the simple question of who to leave them with. There will be busy or travelling spouses, single mothers without live-in nannies, and unsympathetic partners. In *Lean In*, Sheryl Sandberg advises women who want to succeed to choose the right partner. My thought on reading this recommendation was that this was not a key success factor in patriarchal Nigeria. Here, there is a fixed formula for marriage and care giving. For women who want to have it all, it is down to supportive mothers, sisters and friends.

Chapter 6

The Delegate Game

There were two kinds of delegates: automatic and ad hoc. The automatic ones were PDP royalty. They were incumbents and state-level executives, past and present. There were forty-three of them and even before I understood how the delegate system worked, I started out with a list of twenty-nine of them, along with their telephone numbers. Hajiya Ireti who gave this list to me advised that while I waited for the rest of the names, I should start lobbying the delegates for their votes as soon as possible. She mentioned a few that I might not want to bother with; their loyalties were already reserved for incumbents or the highest bidder.

As for the ad-hoc delegates, there were three from each ward. By party rule, at least one per ward had to be a woman. There were twenty-two wards in my constituency: ten in Bwari and twelve in AMAC. In all, I had to engage with one hundred and nine delegates, of whom sixty-six were yet to be elected by their respective ward congresses.

"Have you picked up your delegate form?" Josephine, the auditor of the FCT PDP asked me one afternoon at the end of a meeting with party dignitaries. She was an automatic delegate herself. "Don't you want to be a delegate and at least vote for yourself?"

I gave a half shrug. In fact, I hadn't thought about this possibility.

Josephine advised me to get a delegate nomination form while I considered it and to move fast. Politicians were buying up all the delegate forms. I parted with ten thousand naira immediately. Then tried to find out more about the delegate elections. They were scheduled for 1 November.

There were various ways to acquire a stake in the delegate industry. Serious aspirants bought up as many delegate forms as there were delegates. In gubernatorial elections for example, there could be as many as one thousand two hundred delegates. These aspirants would process the applications by filling them out, paying for passport photographs and ensuring that their nominees were all mobilised to be at the party congress, arranging for transport and incidentals as needed. This was a good option for aspirants with friends on the state selection panels, which were made up of senior party members appointed by the National Working Committee to supervise the delegate selection process.

Another route was for aspirants to draw up a list of proposed delegates for all the wards within their constituency, and submit this list to the PDP national headquarters. If you had close ties to the leadership of the party this approach had promise.

The third option was for aspirants to take their chances with the delegates that emerged from the party congresses. This did not seem ideal, given the other strategies at play, but my network and resources were limited; not to mention the ethical issues.

There was a fourth option. This entailed having people ready to show up at short notice, and having a firm understanding with party officials in charge of the primaries that would allow for substituting the official delegates with impersonators.

As for my own chances of becoming a delegate for my ward, Wuse, I had no illusions. But when I heard ward members were meeting to discuss delegates, I made sure to show up at the Green and White Garden in Wuse Zone 1. Besides, it would be my first ward meeting.

The meeting involved much fancy talk about unity and family. Then the two aspirants – myself and another tall young man, Abdulrahaman, who spoke with an American accent – introduced ourselves. After this, Gajo asked how many of the attendees wanted to be delegates. Eighteen hands shot up. The leadership would make the best decision for the ward, Gajo assured us. He pre-empted complaints by saying those who emerged as delegates, as representatives of the ward, would be required to bring home the treasure so that the family could share.

On the day of the ward congresses, I spent most of the morning and early afternoon at the Imperial Hotel off Adetokunbo Ademola in Wuse 2, where Wuse ward members were supposed to gather. Gajo never showed up, nor did anyone else who wanted to be a delegate. I spent the time talking politics with various party members who were milling around. Some by now were familiar; others were new to me, and most I would never see again regardless of promises made and despite cash for mobilising delegates changing hands.

Later, I called Gajo to find out the results of the congress. He informed me that Wuse's delegates were two women, Hajiya Ireti Kingibe and Martha Okechukwu, and one man, Sanusi Tanimu. He could arrange a meeting with the two people I did not know, but he could not help me with the sixty-three ad-hoc delegates for the other eleven wards.

Clearly, this was going to be a process involving any number of intermediaries. Al-Hassan GwaGwa, a former FCT PDP chairman with the distinction of being the longest serving chairman for the FCT, was one of my options. Amir first introduced me to him and I had kept in touch through GwaGwa's son, Yusuf. I called at least once a week to check on how GwaGwa was doing – he was an elderly man with delicate health – and shared updates about my campaign. On my next call, I told Yusuf that I would be visiting. I needed to ask for GwaGwa's help with the delegates.

It was after Maghrib prayers and raining heavily when I got there. I was in and out in minutes. GwaGwa seemed ready to retire for the night. He shuffled into the living room and settled into what I could already tell was his regular living room chair, a two-seat sofa facing the entrance. It was positioned like a throne. I waited deferentially to sit. GwaGwa was not as positive about my plans as he was when we first met. I learned that he and a few FCT traditional rulers had gone to see President Jonathan to renew their requests for equity in land ownership, an FCT representative as minister, and a share of the federal character quota in the senior civil service.

At that meeting, the president said he had a favour to ask concerning Senator Aduda. He wanted the senator's rivals to be persuaded to step down. Following that meeting, GwaGwa said, some aspirants were invited to a meeting with the FCT minister and asked to withdraw.

"Were you at that meeting?" GwaGwa asked me in Hausa.

"I was not," I replied.

GwaGwa remained silent for what seemed like a long time.

"Then you are still in the race," he said. "If you were not asked to step down then you have no business with them." He smiled for the first time.

I agreed.

At this, he signalled that the meeting was over. There was no promise or next step. I left a consultation fee in an envelope and something extra for Yusuf and left.

Later that night Yusuf phoned me. After I left, he said, his dad had called eight out of twelve AMAC ward chairmen and told them to come to the house after Juma'a prayers the next day. These eight were the ones he knew well and trusted, the ones who listened to him. Yusuf told me I should arrive by 3p.m. The meeting would be to introduce me as an aspirant and get them to pledge their support. In turn, these ward chairmen would arrange for me to see the delegates for their wards. This was exciting. Things seemed to be moving. I called Maryam Ali and asked her to please come along. It would be useful to have Ahmadu Ali's daughter by my side.

When we arrived, all but one of the eight were there. They all sat on the carpet in front of Alhaji Gwagwa. Maryam and I tried to join them on the floor, but GwaGwa asked us to sit on the sofa to his right. We greeted the men and sat.

I had barely switched my phones to silent mode when mounds of hot steaming rice, vats of stew with rocks of chicken and beef struggling for space and platters of coleslaw bombarded the small island created in front of Alhaji Gwagwa. The food was good and I was surprised at how hungry I was. Apart from slight murmuring and the clink of spoons on plates, we all believed in not talking with our mouths full. Once the plates were cleared away, we got down to business. By this time, the eighth chairman had joined us. We were complete: City Centre, Orozo, Karshi, GwaGwa, Kabusa, Jiwa, Nyanya and Wuse.

Alhaji GwaGwa began by telling the ward chairmen that he did not know me, but he knew the person who sent me and he would do anything for that person, who was a man of his word, someone who had been very helpful to him personally and to the people of Abuja in general.

"Chairman Ali sent her to me for help and support, and as your leader, I am asking that you accept and support her."

There were nods and murmurs of approval when Alhaji GwaGwa mentioned Dr Ali's name.

I had moved to the carpet during Alhaji's introduction so that I would be on the same level with the chairmen. When he invited me to address them, I struggled through my Hausa interspersed with English and told them a little about myself.

"I have lived in Abuja since 1996," I began. "It is home to me and my entire family. This is where we married, where we all live and where we have invested in property. It is home to all of us and we care about our communities."

I continued. "I am a lawyer. I studied law because I do not like injustice. And this is the same reason I left the private sector to get involved in working with and for women. And now I want to represent you at the House of Representatives, because I see a lot that is wrong that can be put right. I know what the burning issues of the people of FCT are. They want proper representation, equitable compensation for land and a minister from the FCT. Some of these things will take time but we can do it if we work together. The first step in achieving some of these things is having a representative who will work for your interests. You will have that right away if I am elected."

"Dan Allah, ku bani goyon baya," I beseeched as I sat back from my crouched position on the floor. Only when I leaned

back into my heels and my muscles stopped screaming did I realise that I had leaned forward on my haunches while I spoke.

As chairman of my ward, Gajo was given the opportunity to speak first. He asked the gathering to permit him to give me a proper introduction and share a bit more about my work and who I was. He described me as a passionate, fearless writer who had made a name in certain circles, and told them about my work for the protection of the rights of women and better governance. He asked them to believe him that I was a respected person with a recognisable name and would be a true and effective advocate for the people of the FCT.

It was a really good introduction. I felt pleased and touched. I wondered how I could get him to make introductions like this as I met with delegates and other people I needed to persuade. I learned later that as chairman for a ward, he had to be seen as neutral and could not join me on the campaign trail.

After him, four other chairmen spoke. They asked questions and expanded the discussion on the issues they dearly wanted their representative to address. I had put my finger on some of the issues but there were more — land swaps, economic empowerment, education, more area councils and wards and a mayor for Abuja. They also wanted to know what I planned to do for the rural, still underdeveloped areas of the FCT.

Alhaji GwaGwa was not fooled by the love in the air.

"Everyone has spoken well," he said. "Now when do we arrange for her to meet with your delegates?"

We agreed that the next day, a Saturday, would work fine, and once we finalised the venue, we would let them know. The chairmen for Orozo, Karshi, GwaGwa, Jiwa and Kabusa each committed to bringing all their ad-hoc delegates. Nyaya and Wuse pledged two each. City Center said there were still some contentious issues around his delegates, and asked to be excused until these were resolved. After we closed with a Christian prayer (having opened with a Muslim one), I stood at the doorway leading outside where I thanked the chairmen individually, said how much I looked forward to working with them, and pressed a pre-prepared envelope into each hand.

We had little time to plan for the next day. Yusuf said he would need a down payment for a hall in the Bolingo Hotel. My spend control radar went up. Bolingo? That sounded expensive. Couldn't we find something within town? I thought of the low-key motel off Aminu Kano Crescent in Wuse 2 where I met some members of the Wuse executive committee on the day PDP delegates were being elected. It was popular with party members and bound to be less expensive.

Yusuf was adamant. Bolingo was well known to the chairmen and delegates, and it brought a level of swag that indicated seriousness. I handed over what he said he needed. Internally, I made peace with the fact that for this particular transaction, there would be no receipt.

Part of Yusuf's pitch was that he knew the Bolingo management so well that they would let us bring our own refreshments. I was impressed. Then he called, late at night, to say we would have to pay for the hotel's refreshments after all. I told him to scratch the refreshments altogether. The meeting would not be long. We did not have to serve the delegates and chairmen in the hall; we could have packs of drinks and snacks waiting outside, to offer them as they left the hotel.

Saturday morning was spent coordinating orders of meat pies, donuts and soft drinks, turning my dining table into an assembly line where these items were packed in individual polythene bags.

The room at Bolingo Hotel was in the basement. There were no windows, and not much air. I did not like how it had been set up, with a high table on an elevation, separating the proles from the VIPs.

I found Maryam and Hakeem, who was Dr Ali's chief of staff of sorts, seated at the high table with five others. They beckoned me to my space close to the centre. I walked across the front of the table and greeted everyone. There was one other woman, Amina Haruna, the Woman Leader for AMAC and an automatic delegate. I promptly exchanged numbers with her. When I got to Maryam and Hakeem, I suggested we changed the room setting to something U-shaped, and bring the chairs down from the stage.

They looked at me as if I had sprouted another head. "Ayi, come and sit down," Maryam said, patting the chair next to her.

The meeting took about an hour. The Chairman of Kabusa Ward acted as MC, by virtue of his position as chairman of the AMAC Ward Chairmen's Association. *Chairman na chairmomi,* everyone called him – the chairman of chairmen.

After I was through with my introduction and pitch, I listened. Each delegate reciprocated by sharing their name and ward and the discussions opened up. The Karshi chairman was a hit. At the height of his speech, he turned his back on the high table to tell the delegates that the reward for politics was on earth, not in heaven. He stabbed the space above his head and below his knee to punctuate his point. I gathered later that my mention of the idea of altruism in politics during my remarks had been difficult for him to swallow.

My use of the word *justice* however, went over well.

Many of the speakers picked up on it and mentioned it over and over again. I received a lesson in local history: the draconian law of 1976 that deprived indigenes of their land, and the land swap programme, where people were forcibly moved from land in Jabi, that was worth two hundred million naira a plot, to land that was not worth one hundred thousand naira.

Whether by design or a reading of the mood, the non-indigene delegates were quiet. Soon it was time for someone to offer the obligatory closing prayer. While my campaign team handed out pre-prepared envelopes to the chairmen for themselves and their delegates, I moved quickly to the door in order to greet the delegates individually as they left, shaking hands and handing out my campaign cards. A few remarked about the discussions.

One man asked as he shook my hand, "Where are you from?"

"From Wuse," I responded.

"No, I mean originally," he said.

I smiled and said, "FCT is my home."

A week and a half later, on 18 November, Alhaji Gwagwa repeated the process, gathering six out of ten Bwari chairmen. They too agreed to arrange a meeting with all the delegates, and reach out to the chairmen who did not make the meeting. My offer to cater for this meeting was refused. "Are you saying we cannot afford to feed ten people?" Yusuf asked. Afterwards I showed my gratitude to the women of the house, while Mayowa who had recently joined the team as a personal assistant handed the chairmen their envelopes. Mayowa, my sister's friend was God sent. After she joined I could not imagine how I had managed without her. Mayowa was a real life magician who thrived on impossible deadlines and project managing events.

In preparing for the meeting with Bwari ad-hoc delegates, I tried to incorporate lessons from the meeting with delegates from AMAC. I explained to Jamilu who had recently joined the campaign that I wanted the hall arranged collegially. Isiaka had introduced Jamilu as the ideal person to manage the Bwari delegates. He was in his thirties, educated, newly married and worked as an assistant to the deputy chairman of Bwari Area Council.

He did away with the high table, but I did not get the collegial U-shape I wanted. How hard it is to change the smallest things.

We met in the late afternoon and it was a more relaxed meeting. The chairmen of the Bwari wards sat at the back and let the delegates speak. The complaints were now familiar: bad roads, unemployment, poor representation, being forgotten, not being connected to the power grid and the need for soft loans to finance business dreams. When the general meeting was over, I asked for the women to come closer and so we could "speak to ourselves". We pulled a circle of chairs together while Mayowa and Jamilu distributed envelopes to the men.

I asked the women to tell me their perspective on things and what needed to be done. An elderly woman, at least sixty-five, wanted to boost a business selling second-hand clothes. (I had a fleeting desire to make a joke about branding her things vintage).

Another wanted twenty thousand naira to pick up her business selling grains – rice, beans and garri. She had lost her capital nursing a sick child back to health. Hulera, a fiery, articulate lady from Kawu who spoke only Hausa, complained about her community not being linked to the national grid. The lack of power stymied just about any productive venture, from making and selling *zobo* to grinding beans for *kosai*. Hulera said she did not want handouts, she wanted to earn a living. She talked about injustice in the allocation of resources and how women were always left behind. They were tired of empty promises.

When everyone who wanted to speak had had a say, I told them that some of the issues, such as electricity and roads, were not the direct responsibility of legislators, but legislators could do a lot to ensure that those who were responsible did their jobs. I did not want to lie to them and tell them that voting me in would solve all their personal and community problems. Instead, I could promise that I would amplify their concerns, help them organise to ensure their voices were heard and work with them to get sustainable solutions. I told them to take a chance on a woman for a change. I would not leave them behind.

As we said our goodbyes, two women who were part of the meeting came forward to inform me that they were not delegates, and so would not get a share of the money. Thanks to emergency envelopes, Mayowa could sort them out with a little less than what we had budgeted for each delegate. As we pulled out of the Immaculate Suites, members of the PDP youth wing surrounded us, singing and demanding to be settled. I had started recognising some faces. Mayowa did the needful, and as we drove off I wondered aloud how they knew we were there.

The Bwari delegates followed me around in my head for a few days. With generous application of metrics, you could say that a few of them were middle class. The majority was definitely in the low-income bracket. I would be hard pressed to hire them in the private sector in any role other than guard or cleaner. How had they been selected as delegates? Was it based on anything other than their malleability? If these were the people who were selecting people to run for office and ultimately represent millions, then surely they should be more educated, more financially stable, more inspiring?

Then again, that seemed an unfair line of thought. After all, they shouldn't be excluded from the democratic process by virtue of not being educated, or for being part of the majority that lives at the edge of financial deprivation. On the other hand, what did it mean to leave this important task to the most socially and economically vulnerable, to those most fixated with what they could eat today?

It was clear that many of the delegates felt that politicians rode on them to victory and then turned their backs on them. There was a phrase in Hausa that I had heard politicians use when asking for support, and had in turn used myself a few times: *ba ni goyon baya.* It translated to "carry me on your back". In other words, support me.

Was it a fair relationship? Some politicians, especially those who had won elections, thought it was fair. They paid for the votes, met all the outlandish demands; then after the elections were done, the politicians were finished with the delegates and their constituents in general.

I told the delegates that I understood. People would come and make promises; how would they know that I was different? I told them that when people asked, *Ki na son ki yi suna?* Are you running because you want to make a name for yourself? Or are you running because you want to win? My answer was that I was pleased with my name recognition as it was. I wanted to win. I believed that my country and my immediate community could be better. I wanted to stop wondering how hard it could be for a public officer to impact meaningfully on the lives of people.

Hours after the meeting with the Bwari delegates, I began to receive persistent calls and text messages, always from the same number. When I finally answered, a man introduced himself as Musa. He said it was urgent that we meet. He had important information. He had credible intelligence about the primaries. He could guarantee my victory. I had a separate line for the campaign and could ignore him. But he held Mayowa's line to ransom until we confirmed a meeting with him at the PDP office in Garki on the following Saturday.

I seemed to attract advice the way *shinge* are drawn to streetlights. Either seasoned operatives of the politics industry could smell a novice, or I wore my naivety and uncertainty like a scarf. Possibly both. At any rate, there was always a price tag attached to the tail of the advice.

Musa described himself as a minority stakeholder from Dutse ward where his wife was a delegate. He wanted to share with me the intricacies of the Bwari political landscape. There were implications for my campaign. Jamilu, my campaign manager for Bwari, was one of the special assistants to the vice chairman of Bwari Local Government, a man named Muttawali. I already knew that. They were part of a group who wanted a change in Bwari. To this end, they were working to get Peter Yohanna, the chairman of Bwari, out of their way by having him elected into the House of Representatives.

The delegates had been stacked with non-indigenes to ensure that they were not loyal to the incumbent, but would instead vote for Yohanna. I already knew that too.

Musa was involved in these schemes. That, I did not know.

He came around to his pitch. "With thirty thousand naira for each ward, I will place your posters strategically everywhere and people will vote for you."

"Why do you care if I win?" I asked him. "What is in it for you?"

"We are alike," he replied. "I have seen your profile and we need more people like you. As I said, I am a minority too. We want to have a chance in FCT. And you are a woman and I believe in women. We should give them a chance. My wife is educated but she cannot get a job. People ask me if I will write for my wife during the primaries. I tell them no need for that. She is educated."

I thanked him and said I was sure he would understand that I had to consult with my team and would get back to him. I gave him three thousand naira. "For lunch," I added lamely. I was so distracted by his request, which amounted three hundred thousand naira, that I missed a vital piece of intelligence that he had unwittingly passed on to me.

Another would-be adviser was a guard at the Independent National Electoral Commission headquarters in Maitama who recognised me as I walked through the gates one afternoon. He said he had seen my posters and wished me well. I thanked him and gave him a campaign card and forgot all about the encounter.

Early one Sunday morning he called, and when we established that I remembered him, he said he wanted to see me. I encouraged him in the interest of efficiency to tell me over the phone what he wanted. Apparently, my posters were not strategically located around Bwari; one of the APC aspirants was a lot more visible than I was, but he could remedy that. I thanked him and explained that I had a team who I would instruct to find the location where the APC aspirants' posters were and add mine.

I had engaged with a middle-aged woman named Jamila for weeks before I realised that she was not, in fact, the PDP North Central Zonal Woman Leader. I found this out when she called to find out how I was doing with securing the letters of appreciation from party members that I needed for the screening exercise.

"You can give me one, as zonal woman leader," I said.

No. She was a friend of the zonal woman leader whose name and contact detail I never managed to get from her. But she could still help me, by arranging for one of the youth groups to formally appreciate me, in exchange for one hundred and fifty thousand naira. With that transaction successfully executed, she advised me to let her introduce me to all the influential *sarkis* in AMAC and Bwari. I had not thought about it; only one other person had mentioned introducing me to the *sarki* in one of the wards, but it never happened. Historically, in the areas dominated by the Northern Peoples Congress, the major Emirs had dominated the nomination of candidates in their jurisdictions, but there was scant evidence that traditional rulers had any influence over the FCT primaries. I asked Jamila to write a list of all the *sarkis* we had to see and which delegates or wards they could influence so I could plan appropriately. She never got back to me.

There are generations of families involved in the political industry. I met men whose sons and brothers were in the industry and whose grandsons were in training, being mentored to take up their positions in the family enterprise.

As for new politicians, most had powerful sponsors in their party who could smooth the path to nomination and victory. I was a new entrant with no powerful sponsor, but I had a decent network of contacts that swung open some doors. This position did not protect me from the jobbers.

There were endless offers to help organise meetings with influencers and lobby delegates. Everyone was important. Even past ward councillors from three election cycles ago tried to use their seniority to demand their dues.

I could not turn down all the offers – with no experience, I relied on my untrained gut. Sometimes, I handed over the cash knowing full well that the entire amount was going into the person's pocket, and that the recipient was aware that I knew. It was all part of the industry requirements. When you are playing a game, typically you play by the rules, at least until you figure out the exceptions or you can make your own.

Chapter 7

Strategy And Tactics

The primaries were less than a month away. All these meetings were well and good, but I needed an overall strategy to guide me. Otherwise, I might spend all my time on meetings and consultations with would be patrons and those they sent me to, with all the expenses this entailed, and find myself none the better off at the primaries.

There was a problem. I had no idea what to expect on the day of the primaries. This worried me the way a twisted bra strap does – niggling and painful. The primary election process was obscure and apparently kept that way on purpose. I had heard lots of stories about what happened during party primaries, but what was true?

For one thing, I did not know if the voting process would be secret or open. I could not be certain the ad-hoc delegates I was meeting would be the ones who actually voted at the primaries. There was nothing official yet about the delegate verification exercise, and I was still no closer to securing Ahmed Muazu's endorsement. Could I influence the appointment of the returning officer for the primaries? What would it cost to keep the delegates in a hotel one day and night before the primaries, and would it make any difference? What would be the chain of possession of the ballots? Where would the agents be and how much power would they have? How much could I expect to spend and did I need to raise more money?

My lack of strategic knowledge was not limited to how the primaries worked. I was not even sure if I should maintain a low profile or be visible. According to one school of thought, until I got the endorsement of the party, I should be as quiet as a mouse trying to get past a cat and plastering posters around would only serve to alert the cat. The other view was that I should get in the party's face, blow up social media, and then turn off my phones so that instead of trying to see them, they would come looking for me. "Let them start looking for your mother's number as a means of getting across to you," someone suggested. There was no convincing me that being on Twitter and Facebook made any difference; my delegates were not on those mediums, and I was ready to wager that none of the people I engaged with online would know my delegates and their handlers. I wanted a safe middle with enough visibility, that when I met with party hierarchy, I was in a strong position to make a case for being the preferred candidate.

I held two separate strategy sessions with friends, colleagues in civil society and members of the campaign team and found a sense of direction to plan. This gave control-freak me some peace, a shield against the deluge of advice and a filter with which to assess it.

Really, it boiled down to one question: what did I need to do to get the majority of delegates to vote for me?

The first thing was to identify my base and create one if I did not have one. I wanted the women. There were twelve in Bwari and nineteen in AMAC. Thirty-one out of one hundred and nine delegates was hardly a majority, but it would be a good start.

I wanted non-indigenes. There were at least forty non-indigene ad-hoc delegates out of the total of sixty-six. Fifteen were in Bwari and Isiaka, who had joined my campaign when Yohanna stepped down believed he could deliver them all. With Yohanna out of the race, the campaign team felt I had a better chance than Jisalo of picking up those votes. I also wanted the indigenes in both area councils who were unhappy with Jisalo.

As for the automatic delegates, the general consensus was that I would not be able to sway them. When I asked what our strategy for AMAC would be, I was told, "*AMAC kasuwa ne.*" AMAC is for sale. I could not prevail in that auction. Instead, Bwari was where I would focus for most of my votes.

That gave me a hierarchy of targets. Next, I needed an approach to court them. My options were to host the delegates and visit them and attend as many social events — births, deaths, and marriages — as possible. We agreed that I would start reading the FCT focused newspapers and magazines (a class of publications that I barely knew) to find out what was happening around the city, and I would also have to give delegates their monetary dues.

We came up with a rough estimate of expenses for engagements.

Item/Audience	Cost (N)
Ad-hoc delegates (66)	1,320,000
Automatic delegates (43)	400,000
Ward Chairmen (22)	550,000
Luncheon with delegates (5k per head)	640,000
FCT PDP Office	250,000
Screening	250,000
Total	**3,410,000**

It had become clear from my previous engagements that the way to some of the delegates, particularly in AMAC, was through their patrons. No matter how long and hard I engaged them; they could not take the decision to vote for me.

"I would love the chance to talk more with you," I said to

Martha Okechukwu, one of the two female ad-hoc delegates from my own ward, the first time I met her at Bolingo Hotel. "Speak to Honourable Josephine," she responded as she walked away. I got a similar response, albeit slightly more diplomatic, from one of the City Centre delegates. "Do you know Wulus? You must speak with him."

My plans had to include engaging with delegate influencers.

Finally, there was the question of message. My messages to each group had to resonate. Many non-indigenes were small business owners who faced multiple taxation rates and various obstacles in engaging with the Federal Capital Development Authority and the area councils. An intermediary or broker who would set up structures to ease these relationships would be welcome.

On the issue of roads for the interior areas in Bwari, we agreed that I had to make it clear that responsibility for roads lay with the ministry of works and FCT minister. I could only lobby, encourage and explore creative ways of financing the roadwork required.

I would also have to talk about employment. At a meeting with Bwari delegates, one of them told me that he would give his vote to the person who would get him a job. That was a cue to hire him as a member of my team, but of course the penny did not drop until it was too late. We decided to focus on self-employment. It might not be exactly what people who lived in a government town wanted to hear, but there were opportunities. My responsibility would be to ensure that the residents of FCT got to identify and take advantage of them.

As the primary election got closer and closer, the problem simplified. The central question was now: 'What is each delegate worth and are some delegates worth more than others?'

To get the answer, we sought expert counsel.

We arranged to meet with a former councillor of Wuse and veteran political operative who had managed all Hajiya Ireti's campaigns for the Senate. He told us the story of how Yahaya GwaGwa lost the PDP primaries for the House in 2011 by only seven votes. They had decided to give each delegate fifty thousand naira but the agent in charge of this process – a family member – put some of the money in his pocket and gave the delegates only thirty thousand naira each. Meanwhile Jisalo, who had been lying low, surfaced the day before the primaries and personally gave each delegate eighty thousand naira. Delegates from City centre and Wuse got one hundred thousand naira each.

Al-Hassan GwaGwa felt differently about delegate differentiation. "If you have, give between fifty and eighty thousand naira each," he said. "But you cannot give some less than others, because delegates talk to each other."

I decided that it would be okay to differentiate, if necessary, between the delegates. But the most important message I heard was: don't trust anyone when it comes to money.

I needed at least fifty-six votes to win. This meant we should plan and budget to give the heavy money to at least seventy delegates, to be safe. How to choose these seventy? If we gave all the ad-hoc delegates equally, that took us to sixty-six, but there were automatic delegates who were on my side that I could not afford to ignore.

When Jamilu, Isiaka and I made the final decision about delegate dues, we took the following into consideration: that some delegates would not vote for me no matter what; that Jisalo could and would outspend me (it was expected he would give at least a hundred thousand naira based on precedents set in 2011), and finally, though AMAC was a market for the highest bidder, it also had more sophisticated delegates, and it was okay to gamble that there were some who would vote for me because of who the alternative was.

I would secure Bwari a hundred per cent by attending to every ad-hoc and automatic delegate, and in AMAC I would pick the wards and delegates where there was room for persuasion.

Rumours continued to fly. We've heard tales of grovelling, crying, kneeling, prostrating, horse-trading, reliance on fetishes, illnesses, injections, Ghana-must-go bags, envelopes and caps. Nothing is ever confirmed and there was no way to substantiate a story until it did or did not happen.

One rumour was still circulating: the primaries would not hold. There was a variant. The primaries would take place, but the party was not going to announce the results when the process was completed. Instead, ballots would be taken away, and only the national headquarters would announce winners.

These stories were disturbing. But a tiny part of my brain recognised that there was a perception war going on. Some people would be raking it in from the uncertainty.

One evening, I followed a lead from my brother Sabo and called his friend Tunde who worked with Uche Secondus, the national deputy chairman of PDP. Maybe a meeting with Secondus could get me a meeting with Ahmed Muazu. Tunde drove nails into my contest and told me where to bury it. He said I should forget the whole thing: it was in the president's interest to support incumbents and indigenes during the FCT primaries. "Find a way onto one of the president's re-election committees, work hard, make a name for yourself and prepare for 2019," he advised.

His diagnosis tallied with news reports. Governors and the presidency were in intense negotiations regarding the president's desire for an unopposed bid for a second term. The arrangements were complicated. Some legislators, particularly Senators with gubernatorial aspirations, were not the chosen successors for their states, and were in danger of losing their seats to retiring governors. Primaries would be fierce and result only in more disruption.

None of the anointed successors to the retiring governors were female. Only eight out of the one hundred and nine senators were women, so if all incumbents were guaranteed their seats, how would we get more women elected? How would we improve the diversity and inclusiveness of our highest legislative organ? The formations did not look good for any new entrant into elective politics, and for women in particular.

I put my thoughts on paper and came up with the first draft of an article that summarised these points. In a nutshell, I made the case that by securing his presidential nomination with the promise of automatic tickets; the president was damaging democracy and the party. I emailed the first draft to three people who could serve as sounding boards: my friends, Bolaji and Opeyemi, and Mr Atedo Peterside a renowned banker. I picked Bolaji, a communications expert and Opeyemi, a fellow disrupter because I expected their views would be different. I found Mr Peterside's perspective on issues insightful; we were members of an online group and he often made me appreciate elements of an issue I had not considered.

Bolaji called, sent SMS and blackberry messages non-stop, until I had a chance to speak to her.

"Are you crazy?" She yelled down the phone. "I am begging you. I am begging you. I take God beg you. Please do not publish this article. Don't you know you are part of establishment now?" Her voice rang in exasperation. "You are no longer wearing the cloak of a journalist or activist. You are now a politician."

Ope thought the article was fantastic.

"Send it," he said. "But you know publishing could have two very different consequences." The message in the article could be welcomed by the party leadership as what was needed to bring all the conflicting interests to a negotiation table and give me the visibility and access I wanted. Or, it could be perceived as an indictment on the way the party was handling issues and result in a negative reaction to my candidacy. "Everything you said in the article needs to be said," Ope said at the end of our discussion. "But it does not have to be said by you."

Mr Peterside responded by email and asked if we could speak later in the day. I was having dinner when he called, right on time. We talked for close to an hour. He agreed with everything I said in the article. He advised I send it as a letter to the president, with a request for a response within a period; otherwise I would go public.

He also advised me to copy Ahmed Muazu. He promised to ensure Muazu would get the letter, but confessed that getting me to see the president or Muazu would not work. For the president, it was too mundane a matter, as for Muazu; it was near impossible to see him. And when one did see him, Muazu had little attention to give any one person or issue at any time.

As we drew to the end of the discussion, Mr Peterside asked me if I had a budget for my campaign. I confirmed that I did. "Write a letter to ANAP Foundation asking for support and explaining why you are the better candidate," he said. I am sure you can do that, you write very well." ANAP was Mr Peterside's non-profit organisation. To say I was pleasantly surprised would be an understatement. I would not have felt happier if I had picked up an old handbag and found a wad of forgotten dollars.

I followed Mr Peterside's advice and used the contents of the article as a letter to President Jonathan and copied Muazu and Y.Y. I never got a response but later, Josephine told me that when Y.Y got his copy of the letter he showed it to her. Her verdict: "It is not done to send this kind of letter to the President."

I had to make time to meet with and revisit party leaders on the FCT and ward level, not least since these included current and past executive committee members who were automatic delegates. A few were hostile and I did not want to give them any additional excuses.

A week after I picked up my forms, I had met with the FCT PDP executive committee to introduce myself and ask for their support. Zuby arranged for the meeting in the boardroom of the FCT PDP headquarters. I was nervous about the optics, but Zuby said it was not unusual for aspirants to meet with party members in the office. It would save me the cost of renting a hall and serving refreshments.

We were set up in the boardroom before they came in. I took the opportunity to greet each person individually as they walked in, introduce myself and shake hands. After Zuby's brief opening stating the objectives of the meeting,

I got up, welcomed them in English and Hausa and sought their permission to speak in English.

After describing my personal background and career, I turned to the reasons why I had decided to run.

"There are several reasons why I would like to represent the people of AMAC and Bwari in the House. While my writings reflect some of these reasons, I would like to use a recent experience to capture what drives me.

"A few months ago, I had the opportunity to sit with a group of young girls – unmarried mothers from various parts of the FCT. They were hosted with their babies by Education as a Vaccine, for two days in a hotel at the edge of Life Camp. They were identified as high risk for HIV/AIDs and the workshop was designed to discuss reproductive health and safe sex options. A few shared with us after the first day how fascinated their children were with lit up light bulbs – they could not take their eyes off the lights because this was their first experience of electricity. Some of these young girls were bright and full of ideas, but they could not finish their education for lack of funds and opportunity. Some still lived with parents who thought educating girls was a waste. Many were not involved in any commerce at all. Most of the girls lived in areas largely cut off from the rest of the world during the rainy season because of bad roads. They did not sell recharge cards or pure water, and one who tried to sell *kosai* (fried bean cakes) in the evenings when it was cooler and there was less competition, had to end her enterprise when the village chief advised that her frying at night would attract witches.

Their lives were a portrait of insufficient investment in infrastructure, education and health, government neglect, and abandonment by their representatives. By not equipping them to be self-sufficient in the future, we are sentencing the future generation to a life of poverty.

I know these girls and the people of the FCT deserve a lot more than what they are getting and I would like to contribute to making lives better for as many as possible. Once the lives of women improve, we will see immediate impact on the lives of entire communities."

As I spoke, I continuously scanned the faces of the executives, but got no clues that the story had penetrated their shields of disinterest.

I closed by requesting that they indulge me and share perspectives on what the people of AMAC and Bwari truly want from representatives, and how I could have a successful campaign.

The women were positive. There were five in the room out of the nine executives present. They were pleased that more young, educated women were taking part in elective politics. I found out then that one of the aspirants for the

Abaji-Gwagwalada-Kuje-Kwali constituency, the other House of Representative seat for the FCT was female.

The men were not so constructive. One of the state executives who doubled as a member of the national executive committee asked if I was married and if I had my husband's permission to contest. The chairman of AMAC pointed out that I could not be a serious contestant if I had not been to see him yet. Another man questioned my eligibility to run and asked how long I had been in the party.

My fixed smile mask would have been perfect for a Botox ad.

"You have all spoken well," I murmured when all comments had been exhausted. I begged for the forgiveness of my AMAC chairman and others I had not been to see yet. I acknowledged that I was late in declaring my interest. I was struggling to make up for lost time with group meetings such as these, but would remedy my mistake at everyone's convenience. As for my eligibility to run, I had been a member of the party for a long time. I was guilty of not being active, but I was determined to change that now.

I had already learnt to say as little as possible, instead of defending myself of any accusations. I ended by saying their support would mean a lot to me and to start remedying my neglect of party duties, I was donating one hundred thousand naira to the party. I handed over the prepared envelope to the secretary of the party and thanked them for their time. Later I got feedback that I had acted like a headmistress, lecturing them. Apparently, I should have sat while speaking and not talked so much.

Some evenings Jamilu and Isiaka would come by my house and we would go in one of their cars to visit PDP royalty. This was how we saw Matawalle, the deputy chairman of Bwari, Dogondaji and Yahaya GwaGwa who lost the primaries to Jisalo in 2011. He now worked with the FCT minister in the FCDA. I found the meetings at home uncomfortable. Not because the hosts were unfriendly in any way, but the meetings felt like intrusions, and I was rarely at my most eloquent in that setting. Or maybe it was the time of the day that worked against me. Does sitting in the living room of a person for a few minutes, witnessing interactions with his wife or children, give you an insight into who a person is and what they stand for? What can one tell from the size or location of a house, how clean it is or the arrangement of the furniture and where people choose to sit?

I hosted my ward executives in my home on the Wednesday before the primaries. It had been a complete oversight on my part not visiting my own ward executive committee. Having two people from Bwari as my key campaign advisers did not help my vision. I knew the committee had all heard about my meetings with the delegates and ward chairmen. I explained that I saved the best for last. We sat around my living room enjoying drinks and snacks as I listened to anecdotes and more advice.

The meetings were good for more than just fulfilling requirements and massaging egos. I picked up threads of information along the way that helped me weave a better understanding of the PDP delegate process. In the old system, all the ward executives were delegates. With an average of ten to twelve executives in each ward, and twenty-two wards in the case of my constituency, this came to hundreds of delegates – thousands for those contesting gubernatorial and presidential elections. It was near impossible to meet all the delegates, and when meetings with delegates were arranged they were rowdy and hard to manage. For aspirants, the new streamlined delegate structure was better in terms of connecting with individual delegates. But it had executives feeling left out of the process. And with fewer delegates, the prevailing theory was that payoff stakes would be much higher.

I enjoyed hearing stories from the primaries battlefield and the meetings gave me an opportunity to add to my collection. Sometimes, the moral of the story was clear; more often the stories left me more confused about what my winning strategy should be. In one story, a female senator seeking re-election took three hundred and fifty million naira into the arena on the day of the primaries and came out without one kobo. Before the primaries, she had spent money on cars, motorcycles and all sorts of other incentives. I was shocked when at the end of the story, the senator lost. The person who told me the story wanted to make sure I understood that all the money in the world was futile if the powers that be are not on your side. "Money isn't everything," the storyteller said. Not even in politics where the reward is "here on earth and not in heaven".

Another illuminating story was about Amina Yusuf's experience with PDP during the primaries for one of the three Niger state senatorial tickets in 2011.

When the ballots were counted after the primaries, she was the undisputed winner. The state's first lady, Governor Babangida Aliyu's wife, called to congratulate her. Then the party announced on the radio that the incumbent, Aliyu Nuhu, a former deputy inspector general of police had won. Amina Yusuf did everything she could to bring the theft of her mandate to the attention of the world and the party leaders, but PDP did not budge. Another party, the CPC, invited her to join them, knowing how popular she was in her constituency. Instead, she decided to stay in PDP and undermine the party by working to ensure the CPC candidate won. CPC took the senatorial district and the House of Representative seats too.

The meetings also gave me a chance to address some of the questions delegates and delegate influencers had about my aspiration.

I had to explain a few times why I was running from FCT and not from Kogi. Apart from being an advocate for state citizenship based on residency and birth, I had never lived in Kogi for any length of time. Visits to family over the years did not translate to calling a place home. If all politics is local, then for me the people who lived in a place, who knew its issues and were involved should be the ones to contest from there.

The norm for political candidates in Nigeria is to commute between where they live and their constituency, meeting people and working on community projects. This is not practical for many reasons. There are the treacherous roads and cost of travel and accommodation to consider. For women who are mothers of young children and have little or no co-parenting support, there is also the tension of leaving them every weekend for community engagements. Do you take them along and put them at risk? Do you leave them with nannies every weekend? It makes sense to get involved in politics in the location where you earn, pay taxes and support local enterprise, not where your parents or in-laws grew up decades ago or believe they are from.

There was still another formality to satisfy – screening by a panel set up for that purpose. When I woke up on the morning of 19 November, the first of two days scheduled for screening aspirants, I knew nothing, save the names of those on the panel.

The list of party members responsible for screening PDP aspirants nationwide had been published only the day before. I did not know anyone on the FCT panel. I copied out the names and shared them with a few friends and silent well-wishers within the party. Before I went to bed, one of them called to let me know he knew the chairman of the panel well and had spoken to him about me. I slept soundly with this knowledge.

Rumours were running around and having babies. Now that the party leaders had got rid of Yohanna, those of us they did not want to deal with would be screened out of the primaries. Problem solved.

After the school run in the morning, I made a few calls. No one knew anything yet about the venue, time or procedure. Even the chairman of the panel was in the dark.

Shortly before 11 a.m., information began to filter out. The screening exercise was going to take place at the Nicon Luxury Hotel in Garki Area 10. There was also a form that all aspirants needed to submit. The forms were at the PDP office in Garki, a five-minute drive from the screening venue. My control antennas were tingling. It felt like a set-up.

At the party office, Mayowa and I walked briskly past the praise singers. They made half-hearted attempts to hail us. We were determined not to see them. It was only my second time in the administrative office of the FCT PDP headquarters. Zuby was already there to get the form for Hajiya Ireti, and the occupants of the office were trying to shake him down. Their time had come.

There was an empty chair next to the desk where the man with the forms was presiding and he gestured for me to sit. I tried to determine from the discussions if there was a fee for the form. Zuby was standing at the other end of the desk opposite the functionary. He twitched and snapped as they argued about the necessity of aspirants coming in person to pick up the form. Eventually, Zuby strode out with a bounce and the form in his hand. "Don't give them a penny," he told me in Hausa.

The form was identical to the local government election form Josephine had given me a few weeks ago to help me prepare for the screening process. I skimmed through it as we drove off. There was a section that required clearance from the Code of Conduct Bureau and for about half an hour I was in panic mode calling contacts to determine who knew anyone there. I was still waiting for someone to get back to me when I got to Nicon Luxury and found out that the clearance requirement was only for public officers.

It took the entire day to screen four aspirants for the single senatorial seat for the FCT, and three out of seven aspirants for the two House of Representatives seats. The rest of us spent the entire day there because we did not know if the panel intended to see all the aspirants or some, or if they were seeing us based on our positions on a list. We hung around and chatted and shared the stories we had heard about plans for the primaries.

Senator Aduda was the first person screened. When he was done, he had a small band of people ready at the door to form his entourage. He had to go past us to get to the elevators. He hailed us with arms stretched up and waving. This was my chance to follow up on lots of unanswered telephone calls and text messages. I walked up to him and introduced myself as we shook hands.

"I have been trying to see you sir," I said.

He admitted that a few people had approached him about me, one only the night before. "But I know you," he said. "I have seen you on TV."

I smiled. "I have been trying to reach you to tell you about myself and get your support for my candidacy."

He nodded, but said nothing and began to move towards the elevators. His aide spoke to me instead: "We should talk more." I gave him my card and he recited his number, which I duly stored, never to be used.

By 5p.m., most of us had moved from the lobby area with chairs to the narrow, airless corridor right outside the room where the screening panel was meeting. As soon as Jisalo stepped outside the room, his band rushed to relieve him of his folders. They fell over themselves to shake his hands as if he had just completed a race. His signature smile spread across his face as he looked around and asked, "Who is Ayisha?"

I answered my name and took his offered hand. "I feel like I know you," he said, taking a confident stance with his hands on his waist. "I have seen you before."

I was going to say something witty, but I was getting more adept at sitting on my tongue and quelling instinctive responses. "Thanks Honourable, for accommodating us and letting us participate," I said instead.

"Oh yes, oh yes, there is room for all," he said handing me his card. I gave him mine and he left with his troops.

I understood why Jamila had insisted that I had to be accompanied to the screening. She campaigned for permission to organise supporters who would hail me, but I knew that there would be costs and said no. She shook her head sadly and told me that politicians had to have people around them; otherwise no one would know who they were. I thought it made the politicians and their entourages look clownish. But what did I know?

The legal adviser came out shortly after Danladi Zhin, the former chairman of Kuje Area Council and an aspirant for the House went in. The rest of us had to return the next day, she announced. Would it have been so terrible to inform us earlier in the day?

While people were registering their displeasure, the legal adviser turned to me and said my name was not even on the list of aspirants. She said my file was missing. The puzzle pieces fell into place. Earlier in the day, Amir had called from Lokoja, where he was on the screening panel for Kogi State, to share how shocked he was when my name was announced as the next candidate to be screened. The phone connection had been terrible, and we gave up trying to talk and I forgot all about it.

"Do you have copies of what you submitted?" the legal adviser asked.

I gave myself a mental high five for making duplicates of everything I submitted to the PDP office. I had asked Zuby to ensure the receiving officer acknowledged receipt on the duplicates with the date of receipt.

The next day I went straight to work and told Mayowa to only call me when the person before me was going in.

When I got there, Barrister Ephraim Ushafa, another contestant for the AMAC/Bwari ticket, was being screened and Pastor Toyin Matthews was also waiting. She had not gotten her screening certificate the previous day, because she did not have her birth certificate with her. Her mother had it sent from Lagos by overnight courier.

While we waited, the secretary to the FCT Executive Committee came out and asked solicitously to see my documents. When he saw my tax clearance certificate he asked, "Where are your pay slips to back up your tax clearance?"

I did not have them with me. He stroked his moustache and beard slowly, looked up at the ceiling and back at me.

"You need them. You need proof to show you have been paying your taxes."

"I would not have gotten the clearance without satisfying the requirements," I reasoned.

"You will have problems," he predicted as he walked away.

Down the rabbit hole I went making calls to the Finance & Administration officer at my office and requesting copies of pay slips with tax deductions, asking for them to be saved in PDF format and emailed to Mayowa so she could print them out.

Once I made it into the screening room, no one asked me for them.

The first couple of questions were routine. Why was I running? What value did I hope to bring to the party? Where was the proof of my support to the party? I had paid one hundred and twenty thousand naira for the endorsement from my ward executive committee and with Jamila's thoughtful brokering, another one hundred and fifty thousand to the PDP Youth Vanguard.

Then one of the panelists said, "You have been very critical of PDP. Why did you run on the PDP platform?"

I paused for a few seconds to think.

"I have also been critical of Labour, APGA and APC. I chose to contest under PDP because I have been a member for a long time, just inactive."

The stickiest time was when I thought it was over and was enjoying the banter. The panel members cooed over my framed Harvard certificates that I got Mayowa to bring in during the interview.

"Is this the same Harvard we know?" someone asked.

I had copies and/or originals for everything they asked for. I sat back smugly.

Then someone who had barely spoken asked, "Where is your indigene certificate?"

"I don't have one," I replied, shocked into blurting out the truth.

"But surely if you are claiming to be an indigene, you should have one," he challenged.

I sent up silent thanks for the good sense not to write "Wuse" as my local government when I was filling out the forms. I had debated it in my mind long and hard. In the end, I had written boldly "Kogi State" as my place of origin.

"Sir, I am not claiming to be an indigene," I said. "But because I have lived here since 1996 and this is where I have made my home, I want to represent the people here."

Before he could say another word, the legal adviser cut in. She clarified that there were no constitutional or legal requirements that aspirants or candidates be indigenes. The requirements focused on age, qualification, solvency and soundness of mind, amongst other things.

I could have kissed her. I flooded her with a look of gratitude.

Disarmed, the questioner sat back in his seat. The interview was over. I was told to wait outside and give them a few minutes.

In less than ten minutes, one of them came out to call me in.

"Congratulations," he said as he entered the room with me in tow. "Here is your certificate." He reached towards a colleague who passed it to him and he placed it in my hand.

"Where is our envelope?" he asked casually.

"Here it is," I answered matching his cool. I handed it over and felt a little pleased that they had waited to give me the certificate before making the request.

Chapter 8

On The Campaign Trail

Because Bwari weighed heavier in my calculations to win than AMAC, we decided to start the tour of the wards with Bwari. We determined what we wanted from the visits and what we needed to bring along. This meant one hundred thousand naira for the Bwari executive committee; ten thousand naira for any Bwari ward chairman who attended; and between five and ten thousand naira for the woman and youth leaders, also on the committee. I wanted to send the right verbal and non-verbal signals that would resonate with figures of the local establishment, particularly the automatic delegates. We would find out who had recently had babies, and prepare boxes of Pampers, along with gifts of fabric for the wives, sacks of rice and envelopes too.

We could not stroll into Bwari and talk to the delegates. There were matters of etiquette to follow. First, we needed the blessings of the Bwari Area Council Chairman, Peter Yohanna. Then, we notified the Bwari party eminences of our plans to visit Bwari through Hassan Jehzi, the Bwari PDP Chairman.

We met Yohanna on a Monday morning at the Area Council office. I was impressed. The architecture was perfect for a country with epileptic power supply. There were long corridors with strategic openings and lots of windows, which allowed for natural light and ventilation. There was a clean courtyard with umbrella trees and shrubs that looked well-tended. Compared to the AMAC Area Council offices, the place looked like the grounds of the Taj Mahal.

We sat for ten minutes by a secretary's desk right outside Yohanna's office. I could tell when he approached. Feet shuffled fast and wood and metal chairs screeched across the concrete floors as their occupants jumped to attention. Yohanna bounced in followed by seven other people. "My sister," he said, waving me toward him.

As he lowered himself into his seat, he commented on my youthfulness. He was glad that we were of the same generation, and that younger people were coming forward to contest.

I thanked him for his hospitality and asked for his blessing to go around Bwari and meet with the party structures and delegates. "Bwari is home to me," I said. "I was part of the first set of students called to the bar in the Bwari Campus of the Nigerian Law School in 1998. That was long ago, when we had only one campus for the entire law school. So please do not consider me a stranger. I know

Bwari well." I was relieved that nobody called my bluff by asking me specifics about Bwari localities.

Then the Bwari Area Council members in the room introduced themselves. As we got to the only other woman in the room, I went up to give her a hug and greet her specially. This triggered the obligatory quip from Yohanna about affirmative action. The men roared with forced laughter. We exchanged cards and left. It was all over in twenty minutes.

Jamilu and I proceeded to the party office. It had its own yard with generous space. A large tree provided the only shade in the compound. The entrance to the bungalow led directly into the largest room in the building, which was set up like a magistrate's courtroom, with rows of wooden benches facing a small table with three chairs, and an even smaller table to the side. We sat there for a few minutes with the chairman and then he invited us further inside. A short dark corridor led into a room that was bare of anything but one table and a few plastic chairs. Extra chairs were brought in so we all could sit.

I was surprised at how threadbare the place was. There was not a shred of paper anywhere, no files, books or copies of the party manifesto, posters or stickers. Apart from the PDP flag flying in the yard, and a few campaign posters on the outside gate, there was no sign that it was the PDP party office for Bwari Area Council.

The meeting started when a few more people strolled in, a mix of Bwari ward chairmen and party committee members. As the room filled up, the crowd outside the office also grew. Soon the noise from outside threatened to drown out what we were saying inside. Jamilu and others kept asking them to keep it down. It was the youth league; they were standing right outside the windows, and with no netting or shutters, we could see each other clearly. As I spoke they would intermittently shout – *Sai kin yi, Sai ta yi, Sai mai dankwali.* "You must contest. She must contest. Only the one with the scarf."

I kept my pitch short. I was learning that people liked the opportunity to talk more than they wanted the chance to listen. After I finished my introduction, covering why Abuja was home and why I wanted to represent them, a few party members spoke.

The issues they raised were familiar: they wanted improvements to bad roads, state status for the FCT (and all the perks this would bring to a handful of people), greater access to water, electricity and health care. They complained that the Bwari people were completely cut off from representation as every Senator and House of Representatives member for the AMAC/Bwari constituency, past or present, had come from AMAC. This was why they had put forward their own person, Peter Yohanna.

We wrapped up with a prayer and the room broke into various groups to share the proceeds of my visit. I made a beeline for the only other woman. She had introduced herself as an ex-officio member, and I made a mental note to find out what that title meant. I asked her about the woman leader and she confirmed what I had been told, that the woman leader had a prior appointment. I gave the chairman an extra envelope of five thousand naira to pass along to the woman leader, and gave the youth leader, another five thousand naira. Later, Jamilu would advise me never to leave money for someone who was not there. So, I was pleasantly surprised when I got a call later in the day from an unknown number; it was the Bwari PDP Woman Leader thanking me for the message she received.

Getting out of the building, we had to avoid being mauled by the twenty or so young men who had gathered outside. They refused to budge despite the playful calls from the party executives for them to make way. Beyond the dancing, singing and shouting youth, our car hire driver started the engine. One of Jamilu's people held open the car door closest to the exit. On his signal, I sent a rain of mint naira notes to the opposite side, so I could dash to the car as they scurried for cash. It was my first time spraying naira, which was more popular at owambe parties. It worked but some of them still clung to the car windows and trailed us until we got past the gate.

It was another few weeks before I started my tour of the ten Bwari wards because I needed to raise a bit more money for the visits. On 25 November, I visited seven wards: Kuduru, Bwari Central, Ushafa, Usuma, Byazhin, Kubwa and Dutse. My shock at the condition of the party ward offices soon wore off. In most places, the ward offices were central, within markets or town squares; ideal locations that came with piss-smelling corridors and festering gutters. The offices themselves were little more than one room corner shops with two metal floor-to-ceiling doors, and often, no windows. Dusty and neglected, the offices had no furniture. It was clear the chairs were rented for my visit. I felt bad about the twenty thousand naira we had budgeted for each ward; it would barely offset the rentals and transport fare for executive committee members. The Dutse ward office was the best. It was purpose built with two rooms, but it too lacked tables, chairs, shelves, books, paper, files and pamphlets. None of the offices were set up to register new members, or to keep members engaged and informed, or whatever else a ward party office should do.

It helped explain how difficult it is to register with a political party. The parties do not want people walking off the street and joining. Instead, they want those who are vested in the current structures, are already in political office, or are headed that way. For the latter, the party leaders and assorted godfathers take care of registration through back channels. The parties also seek people who will make the perfect delegates – underemployed, poorly educated, related to members of the political industry, and ready to wait patiently for years to become a councillor or chairperson, and maybe with extreme humility and loyalty, work their way into the state or national assembly.

The primaries were only eleven days away, but the ward chairmen and delegates told me that I was the first aspirant to visit their wards. They were touched by my visit, and a little incredulous at how blatantly the other candidates had taken them for granted. In Bwari Central, the chairman told a group of executives of various ethnicities – Yoruba, Igbo, Hausa, Gbagyi – that the times called for them to move beyond indigene politics, since their own had done nothing for them. The room was barely large enough to fit in two twin beds, but he spoke at the top of his voice, as if he wanted the current representation in the national assembly to hear him. As we walked to the car, Jamilu vibrated and crackled like a pan of hot oil. The chairman's reference to indigene politics was a huge endorsement of my candidacy.

I enjoyed myself. In a way, it felt as if I was in a movie set, something temporary and make-believe. As we moved through the wards, I noted the words and phrases in Hausa and English that got the most positive responses and used them repeatedly. I called the ward executives the "engines behind the delegates". It worked every time; they bobbed their heads in assent, like lizards. They appreciated my references to the party structure being like a family, and my desire to belong.

Byazhin ward left my eyes stinging. We met at the PDP ward chairman's house. The way leading there – you could barely call it a road – consisted of a network of deep ridges and gullies through which foul-smelling, putrid green sewage flowed. We had to walk up a steep incline, and attracted a small entourage of curious people as we went. By the time we got to the house, there were forty people around, only twelve of them committee members. The rest were women and children who wanted to watch. My slow reflexes did not disappoint me; only later did it occur to me that I had missed a chance to connect with the public. I should have greeted each woman individually with a handshake. Instead of money, I should have given the children sweets.

Next day, we hit the remaining wards – Igu, Kawu and Shere. I had been advised to hire a Toyota Hilux or some kind of four-wheel drive due to the condition of the roads. I doubted this advice, how bad could the roads be in the federal capital? I was wrong. The roads were awful. At the end of the tour I felt as if my back and shoulders had been pummelled with a pestle. The worst stretch was from Igu to Kawu; the red dirt road was lacerated with long ridges and fissures deep enough for an adult to lie in. During the rainy season, the residents were cut off from the rest of the world. During the dry season, the traffic moved at a crawl, giving thieves the opportunity, once it was dark, to relieve travellers of their property.

There was an uncompleted bridge along the way with a plaque commemorating the start of construction, sometime between 2003 and 2007. As we drove past the bridge and into Kawu, the scenery evoked clips from old Clint Eastwood westerns – dusty, deserted, and forgotten places where people peered out of windows when strangers came into town.

Igu and Kawu had no electricity because the villages were not connected to the grid. Electricity poles without wires stood at attention alongside the dirt road. They had been hoisted years ago, with nothing else since. Mobile phones got sputtering signals. In Igu, our first stop of the day, there were no cars in the village, save ours. A delivery truck drove in a bit behind us, carrying building and other supplies.

As we finished in Igu, women and children came out to watch us say our goodbyes and take a few pictures. This time Mayowa and I were better prepared; we distributed sweets and almost caused a mini riot. Mothers stretched out their hands and pushed months-old babies in our face, insisting that they too wanted their sweets. To Mayowa's chagrin, I gave the women an unbudgeted four thousand naira to share. I did the same in Kawu.

In Igu and Kawu, we heard again about bad roads, absent electricity, dilapidated schools and clinics (one with its roof blown off), lack of access to potable water, and the empty promises of politicians. "We have tested our people; they have failed us," someone said.

In Shere, the party members were more vocal: *"Za'ayi za'ayi ya ishe mu,"* they said. "We are fed up with: 'we will do this, we will do that.'" The ward chairman explained that Shere was always part of the calculation for winning elections, but once elections were over, they ceased to exist. When locals tried to complain, for instance the time they held a press conference to bring attention to their plight, they only earned the ire of their representative in the national assembly.

Sometime into his third year in the House, Jisalo finally came to visit Shere. The young people barricaded the dirt road and refused him and his sacks of rice access to the village, asking him where their promised modern roads were. After that, he swore that he would have nothing more to do with the people of Shere.

The stories were consistent. Bwari wanted change in representation, and not having Yohanna in the race improved my chances. The other two aspirants in the primaries were not going to be a threat. On our way to Kawu, Jamilu and the ward chairman who had accompanied us for the Igu visit discussed the failed attempt by Abdulrahaman, one of my competitors, to visit the wards a few weeks ago. Apparently, Abdulrahaman had asked one of the Bwari ward chairmen to arrange a meeting of the executive committee and when he finished meeting with them he walked away without giving them anything.

"Maybe he doesn't have money for that," I volunteered.

"*Sai ya hakura,*" said Jamilu. "You don't call people together, get them to leave what they are doing and not give them anything for their trouble. It is not done."

"The only time you do not give a delegate money is when you do not see him," said the chairman, summing it up.

The executive committee members were not happy with the PDP. The guidelines for the primaries, which lowered the number of delegates from past exercises, reduced the influence of the executives. One of them asked, "If only three people were allowed to vote during the general election, would they win?" A few admitted that the new system reduced the cost burden on aspirants. But the consensus was that this would make little difference in the end, because the cost per delegate would go up, as delegates would have to share their proceeds with the excluded executives.

There was praise, however, for Senator Khairat Gwadabe and her boreholes. According to them, she remained one of the best representatives they had known, and many of the projects she initiated still provided value. In many communities across AMAC and Bwari Area Councils, the people I met were genuinely happy that a woman was contesting. They prayed for another like Senator Gwadabe, and many used her tenure as evidence that women are more caring and loyal.

"In mace ta ce za ta yi; za ta yi." Women keep their promises. As we returned to the city, I sent a text message to the former senator to tell her that she was still remembered. I thanked her for being a good role model for women and non-indigenes to follow.

During my run, I did not experience any overt hostility or reservation from delegates and ward-level party officials due to my gender. This was encouraging, up to a point. But the fact remains that gender still weighs against the success of women in politics in Nigeria, particularly in the North where women received the right to vote twenty years later than women in the South. The many obstacles to women's success in electoral politics are further complicated by the raison d'etre of politics in Nigeria – how our public service is structured to operate, which is not to serve but to plunder. Letting women (or anyone new and untested) in would mean reducing the treasure or worse, upsetting the status quo. This unacknowledged frame is the toughest barrier of all.

If women in the North were winning elections to local councils in the late seventies, thanks to the advocacy of people like Mallam Aminu Kano, it is hard to explain why no woman has been elected as a federal or state legislator in Katsina, Jigawa, Sokoto and Zamfara since the return to civil rule in 1999.

At least forty-three women across the world have led their countries as elected heads of state or heads of government. This is worthy of recognition, but compared to the numbers of men who have ruled, the numbers are paltry. In 2016, despite most predictions, the United States blinked when it had the chance to elect its first female president. There is an underlying sexism that is partly connected to the masculinisation of leadership attributes, but it does not stop the political actors from engaging with female politicians who are playing by the rules.

It was soon time to deal with the city part of the constituency, the AMAC wards. In preparation, Jamilu and I met with a party official for Jiwa Ward. "Ay, AMAC *kasuwa ne*," he told us. "If you call members of the executive committees, and ask them to leave their jobs or businesses, they will expect at least thirty thousand naira each." It was not hard to convince me not to bother trying to see them all. It would be best, for budget and expectations, if we restricted ourselves to the ward chairmen and the delegates. Besides, Jisalo had not even bothered to put up posters.

We began our tour of the twelve AMAC wards with Jiwa, GwaGwa and Kabusa. In Jiwa, the ward with the second highest number of registered voters, after Garki, we met three ad-hoc delegates: Amina Haruna, the woman leader and an automatic delegate, the ward chairman and the secretary. There was some trouble getting the key to the office and so we sat outside. Thankfully, there was an awning and it was a breezy day.

The road to Kabusa, which lies beyond Sunnyvale Estate, one of many housing developments outside the city centre, was beyond bad. I could not bring myself to imagine it in the rainy season. Surely only trucks and four-wheel drives could survive? Ibrahim, the chairman of Kabusa, who was also the chairman of the association of PDP ward chairmen, spoke prophetically about my candidacy and what it could mean. I was genuinely moved. *"Gani ya kori ji,"* he began. "Seeing is believing. We know a successful farmer from their preparation of the land." He praised me for taking time to visit them and said it was obvious that I jealously guarded my relationships. He said he knew this because I was the first aspirant to visit, and I had insisted that they put up my poster in the dark windowless room that served as their office, to keep company with the lone faded candidate poster from four years ago.

We took a few pictures outside the office and handed out sweets to three children who were playing near us. I took economical breaths because of the putrid open gutters and streamlets, deep green and bubbling, that streaked across the red caked sand. As Ibrahim walked us back to the car, he said, "We don't want a rep who will forget."

The next day was Saturday. We began at 8.30a.m. and visited Karshi, Orozo, Karu, Nyanya, Garki and City Centre. I had never been to Karshi and Orozo wards, which lay behind Karu. The landscape was beautiful: rocky, green, and aloof. It reminded me of the drive from Cape Town to Stellenbosch. All that was missing were the vineyards. I thought, for at least the hundredth time, about the unexploited opportunities for tourism and recreational activities that lay at the base and at the top of Abuja's rocks. A soldier at a military checkpoint noticed the custom made PDP bags and posters in the back of the jeep when we slowed down and shouted, "PDP! Chop alone; die alone!" We all roared with laughter.

At each stop we gave five yards of brocade to each male delegate, six yards of atampa to every female delegate along with money in envelopes for sewing, plus something for the chairmen.

Some delegates assured me that this was the time of the non-indigene. Others, while declaring me certain to win, volunteered to whip up votes in the wards I was doubtful about.

In places where our analysis showed that we could not expect any votes, such as Gui, Garki and Karu, we kept our visit as brief as politely possible. In the AMAC wards far from the heart of power, the delegates were still mostly of the malleable variety. The mandatory woman, to meet the 'at least one female delegate per ward' requirement, was typically the wife or mother of someone in the political industry.

As we left one ward and headed to the next, we updated our tally of possible votes. There were three in Karshi, two in Orozo, none from Karu, where Senator Aduda was from, two in Nyanya (where one of the delegates was a friend of

Jamilu and Isiaka), none from Garki, where Jisalo was from, and one in City Centre.

The most enlightening conversation took place in City Centre, home of polling unit 001, which we saved for last. We met the one delegate, Charles, who was available to receive us at his home. He enthralled us with his experience of being a non-indigene and his theory that the primaries were going to be determined by the indigene and non-indigene factor in FCT politics.

When our discussions with Charles ended, I asked the City Centre chairman to extend my greetings to the two other delegates, and left their gifts with him. As we filed out of his living room, Charles asked, "Do you know Wulus?"

"No, I'm not sure that I do," I replied.

"You must see him," he replied. "Call him. Tell him I said he is the one person you have to talk to about FCT politics. Go and see him."

Chapter 9

Wooing The Women

When you spend enough time around female politicians in Nigeria, you develop the sense that few of them attribute their success to the women's vote. Sometimes the politicians ask where the women were when the politician was looking for money for her forms, getting harassed by thugs, or fighting to regain their mandate. But more often than not, in a country where everything flows to the source of power, women who were serious about getting elected knew the power resided with men. In turn, women in the general population complained that women in office "do nothing for them", while the women in office view those complaining with a mix of pity, disdain and amusement.

I understood these patterns, but I did not want to fall into them. I was determined to seek support from all the women who I knew could help. Thankfully, I had no need for tools to clear a path to their doors. Some of them, I had to see regardless of my doubts about their willingness or ability to assist. There was always hope for a pleasant surprise, a door unexpectedly flung open.

I knew going to see Dr Chikwe, the PDP National Women Leader, would be as useful as sunscreen on a black goat. Still, when a friend made arrangements for me to see her through one of Dr Chikwe's daughters, I went ahead anyway. I had attended meetings with her and other women leaders of political parties in the past, and knew that we did not agree on much. Dr Chikwe was of the "follow the first lady" school of thought. I had also come to know that women leaders had little power within political parties. Not one single politician male or female, had advised me to see the woman leader of my party when discussing strategy. When I campaigned on the ward level, I had to engage the ward level women leaders, but this was more in their capacity as delegates, not as politicians or party officials with any influence.

On the day Dr Chikwe's daughter and I agreed to meet at her mother's office, I sent a text message in the morning confirming our date. No reply. I called her about noon and there was still no answer. That was my cue not to make the 2p.m. meeting. Instead, I struggled into PDP National Secretariat at Wadata Plaza, on what had to be the worst day to be there. Umar Nasko, the PDP gubernatorial aspirant from Niger State, was at the secretariat to submit his forms to the National Organising Secretary. There were at least three hundred people with him. They were drumming, singing, shrieking, and generating sweat, all intent on getting through the gates as part of his entourage.

When I made it to Dr Chikwe's office, I learnt she was at the presidential villa. I explained to one of the ladies in her office that her daughter had arranged the meeting. She asked if I had called Dr Chikwe. I said I had called and sent SMS, but only the latter was true. I asked if there were any plans to meet with aspirants and she said no. I left, escaping the madness through a back exit. By then the pressure at the gates had eased and I could depart a bit more elegantly than I entered.

The experience with PDP's national woman leader and her daughter, who never returned my call, reminded me of the silence of the Abuja Feminist Forum after a friend, Wunmi, made a kind announcement to the Forum's mailing list about my bid to contest, saying it would be great to support me. Only one person responded. When Wunmi had shared her plans with me, I had been tempted to tell her not to bother. It is nice to periodically prove your suspicions; it builds trust in your intuition.

There were a few women within civil society that I shared my progress and struggles with. One of them was Hajiya Saudatu Mahdi of the Women's Rights Advocacy and Protection Alternative. She introduced me to Isiaka who became an asset to my campaign. We three even spent one evening at Hajiya Saudatu's house coming up with parts of my delegate engagement strategy.

As the rumours grew stronger of aspirants being screened out of the process, I shared my fears with her. We were twenty-three days away from the primaries and I was no closer to meeting Ahmed Muazu and Bala Mohammed to get their support.

One morning, not long after we spoke, Hajiya Saudatu called and told me to rush to Iyom Josephine Anenih's house immediately. Iyom, PDP's first national woman leader had also served as a minister of women affairs from 2009 to 2011. She cared about equal opportunities for women and worked closely with advocates for increased participation of women. She also sat on the advisory board of the Women's Fund. My clothes from the day before were handy and appropriate for my unwashed body. (Being a politician tip number one: always shower at night, you have no idea how early and quickly you will have to leave your house; tip number two: keep bottles of perfume in strategic locations such as your car and handbag.) As I sped towards Gwarimpa, I made phone calls rearranging my morning – lining up a cab to manage school runs and rescheduling a meeting with Alhaji GwaGwa. It was not yet 7.30a.m.

As I drove down the last three hundred meters to Iyom's house, I wondered which members of the PDP leadership I would find in her living room.

There was no one there. I set my travel mug of tea beside me, sent Iyom a text message to let her know I had arrived, and checked my messages. A few minutes later, Ify, an aspirant for the Imo State PDP gubernatorial ticket, came in and joined me. As we exchanged stories we'd heard about the primaries, a young lady came in and told me Iyom was ready to see me. I followed her upstairs and stayed for over an hour.

For lack of a better way to describe the discussion, it was a mentoring session. Of sorts.

"How are you managing with the meetings? Who have you seen?" she asked.

"I have met with a few of the ward chairmen and some of the delegates. Alhaji Alhassan GwaGwa, the former PDP Chairman for FCT, has been very supportive and has helped arrange a few meetings."

"That's good. Who else?"

"I have not seen any of the key people. Not Bala Mohammed. Not Muazu. Not Aduda." As it happened, this was the day I had to go with a UN delegation to see Muazu, not as a candidate but as an advocate for increased representation of women in elective posts. It would not be the right time to seek his support.

She asked me not to give up and said she would try to take me to some people at the national secretariat. There was no specific plan. Then she shared her own experiences. She talked of interminable late night meetings that serious politicians had to ensure they were part of in order to contribute to decision-making. She gave me a pack of wipes to keep myself fresh.

As she recounted the screening of candidates in Delta State and negotiations with party leaders in Ondo to save a few seats for women in the state assembly, I was conscious the minutes were slipping away. I had been wondering how to break the flow of conversation, when the impatience of another guest waiting downstairs, rescued me. I thanked Iyom and rushed out of the house – it was almost 9.30 a.m. It was going to be a hectic day.

In addition to the UN visit to Muazu at the PDP secretariat, my campaign team had made plans for me to meet with all thirty ad-hoc Bwari delegates in their home turf.

When the meeting with Muazu ended, I rushed out, eager to get on the road to Bwari. But as I walked down the corridor leading to the door out of the chairman's wing, Ms Onibon, who was part of the advocacy team, pulled at me.

"I think you should wait and see Dr Chikwe with us. We are going to have a private meeting with her now."

I stopped and stared at her in silence.

"Just my advice, considering what she said inside the chairman's office," she explained.

"You are right," I said. "I will wait with you to see her."

I had rescheduled the meeting with delegates from 1p.m. to 4p.m. I could safely kill another forty-five minutes, but I wanted to get going. The later I arrived, the longer the day would be for all concerned. But it was advice; and somehow I could not pass on it. After Dr Chikwe's public accusation that I had not taken the proper channels to reach the PDP national chairman, I wanted to see if she would remember that I tried to see her.

Dr Chikwe admitted that her daughter had told her about me. She said her response was that I was not running, because I had not come to the national secretariat to make friends.

"You are not making noise," she said. "Nobody knows you. You should be here, seen in the corridors, in people's offices. Everyone knows the incumbent and they know the challenger in Bwari." She was referring to Peter Yohanna. "He has been around making friends, getting support. You know women have to work harder than the men. Nothing is going to be handed to us on a plate and nothing is going to change. We have to play the game like the men."

Late night meetings were never going to stop, Dr Chikwe said. She attended every one, including the ones to which she was not invited and she got there early in order to get a good seat and ensure decisions were not taken without her input and knowledge. National women leaders are part of the national working committee of political parties, but stories of them having to bring their own chairs to events and meetings, because seats are rarely reserved for them, are part of women-in-politics lore. You need the skin of a rhinoceros to be in politics, yet somehow all these thick-skinned people act prickly and sensitive to criticism from the public. Pure batty.

"At the same time, you must ensure you are close to the people," Dr Chikwe said. She related how she did this in her own constituency – visiting often, and sending contributions for events she could not attend. "Women have to know that just coming to national is not enough. The people in the grassroots must like you. It is only when you have their support that national can help. And you have to be strategic."

She was now speaking to me directly. "You have to see Muazu again and get some commitments," she said. "See, like this meeting today, what commitments have you got from the chairman? None. If you had come to me first, we would have been able to strategise, and then we go in there and get something firm."

I nodded my head at the appropriate moments, taking

cues from the murmurs of assent in the room. I did not speak and no one was offended. It was a lecture, not a conversation.

When the meeting ended, I was first through the door already calling Mayowa to meet me at the gates with the car. As I passed through the outer door, I heard Ms Onibon asking for a group photograph and Dr Chikwe telling them some other time.

It seemed that this exhausted my access to big women. The clock was ticking, and I needed to focus on my delegate tally. Getting as many of the women delegates as possible to vote for me – ideally, all of them – was crucial to my strategy.

I invited all thirty-one female delegates to lunch at my house the Tuesday before the Saturday primaries.

We set up outside with tents, chairs and tables. Mayowa arranged individually packed meals of rice and chicken that would be easy to share and take away. There were drinks and snacks to go round several times. A few of the women came with babies and toddlers. Some came with men. This was contrary to my invitation, but I learned that some of the men were the female delegates' guides – they would not be able to find their way home without them. I got Jamilu to escort the men out of the compound and across the road, where we sent them refreshments.

I was not sure if we would get enough attendees. Hajiya Ireti was scheduled to meet with the AMAC delegates at her house that morning and we thought it would be perfect for the women to come over directly from hers. Jamilu was responsible for ensuring that Umar Farouk, Hajiya's campaign manager, would direct them to my house when they were done. The situation was being monitored every thirty minutes by Hajiya Zainab Maina's protocol officer. The minister of Women Affairs and Social Development was the special guest of honour and could only arrive when the event was well under way.

By 2.30p.m., there were enough delegates to address. I broke the ice by welcoming them and telling them how much it meant to host them at home and not in a hall somewhere. I shared a bit more about myself, where I went to school, why I was motivated to contest and introduced my family members present. I told them I needed their support; I knew that I could not win with only the votes of women, but I did not want to take the votes of women for granted. Women were the ones who were being left behind. We could achieve more if we worked together to ensure that when decisions were being made, we were well represented.

I kept it short and passed the microphone around so that those who wanted to speak could do so. A few spoke haltingly, others with more confidence. They praised me for inviting them to my home, for singling them out for special treatment, and promised that they would not shame me. The feisty Hulera, who had impressed me with her eloquence and analysis of the economic situation of women the first time we met in Bwari, raised the issue of broken promises. They were tired of them. They wanted those they voted into power to engage with them all the time, not just during elections.

My sisters, Tosin and Hadiza, and a few friends were there to support me, and helped to chat up the delegates. The music in the background gave the party an informal air. While we waited for Hajiya Zainab, I moved between tables talking with the delegates about what they did to earn money, what they thought about the state of their communities and schools, and how they juggled priorities.

In the end, twenty-three out of thirty-one attended. Our special guest of honour made it with an entourage of two women. She gave a boilerplate speech with the usual references to pray for our leaders, and the other women made some remarks as well. The photographer we had engaged for the event took pictures and printed them on the spot, so that delegates could take souvenirs home. The only blip came when one of the automatic delegates, a current member of the PDP FCT executive committee, made a show of not joining in the group photograph with the minister. The minister took it in good spirit and asked to see her privately so they could talk about her grievance. The woman was unhappy that after the minister rode on their backs to become a delegate for the presidential primaries in 2011, she forgot all about them.

On her way out, Hajiya Zainab handed me one of those black plastic bags that banks put money in – her donation to my campaign. The unexpected gift was like finding a bag of still fresh Kit Kat at the back of the cupboard. That the minister turned up was a kind gesture; I knew it would not tilt the wind in my favour at the primaries, but it was part of the courtship of the female delegates. Her gift would help with the envelopes we had prepared for our guests.

As Hajiya Zainab got into her car, I handed her a small gift of Vlisco Super Wax fabric, thanked her and wished her luck on Saturday – her son was contesting the primary election in Adamawa for the House of Representatives. As she drove out with her entourage, I wondered what my neighbours, the small army of young and middle aged men who sell cars, recharge cards, shayi and suya under the watchful protection of the Abuja Environmental Protection Board, thought about all the commotion.

Chapter 10

Prayers And Intercessions

As the primaries drew closer, offers for prayers increased. Most were made in the normal way that we weave religiosity into everything in Nigeria: "I will pray for you", "We are praying for you", and "God is in control". Those I accepted as my due. My mother and all her friends were praying. The Imam at the mosque she attended was also praying, my friends were praying, and so was I. It was sensible and pragmatic – work hard and pray hard.

A few of the offers, however, were not of the typical variety.

One evening Adamu, one of the drivers we used regularly on our campaign tours, asked how the campaign was going as he drove me home. The key was the delegates and party leaders, I answered. I was comfortable discussing the challenges with Adamu; he was part of the campaign team. He was helpful, had a pleasant and accommodating disposition, and more than once had volunteered to take campaign posters home to paste in his neighbourhood.

Now he asked if I had commissioned any prayers. I confessed I had not given it a thought. Adamu said he knew someone who could organise almajiri prayers. *Almajiri?* I thought I had not heard correctly. The prayers of almajiris were potent, Adamu explained. People with needs regularly arranged for almajiris to pray for them. Into the silence that followed he said there would be no upfront cost, only a promise that he could discuss with the procurer of the prayers.

That scared me even more than if he had asked outright for brown, black and pure white goats. Forget Nollywood; Nigeria has a rich narrative around the role of magic, voodoo and rituals in politics and governance. The thought of being under obligation to repay some undisclosed debt in the future was too much for me. I murmured something vague and pretended to take a phone call by dialling myself from my other phone. When Adamu reminded me of his suggestion a few days after, I told him I had it handled.

The second offer came from a complete stranger. As the lunch with female delegates at my home wound down and I scurried around trying to say personal goodbyes, Mayowa told me that one of the drivers who brought in some of the Bwari delegates wanted to see me. I was standing by the front door and he was only a few steps away so I said, "Of course," and asked Mayowa to get me an emergency envelope. After we greeted each other, the man said he asked and was told I was a Muslim.

Was I indeed a Muslim? I said I was. He said he could tell that I was a good person. I was not immune to flattery and nodded encouragingly. He told me that he appreciated what I was doing with these women but I should forget it; the Christian delegates would never vote for me. I was wasting my time, and what I needed was saukan Quran. This meant reading all 114 chapters and 6,234 verses from the beginning, Suratul Baqara to the end, Suratul Nas. The recitation typically took a few hours with several men reading simultaneously. At the end of the recitation, at least one ram is slaughtered as sacrifice.

My smile was genuine. Adamu had prepared me. I told the man that he was right about prayers, and I had it covered already. I was grateful for his offer, and asked that he kindly include me in his daily prayers. I matched my expression of gratitude with the envelope I put into his hands. He thanked me and left. He called my campaign line a few times to check on me and confirm I had not changed my mind about his offer.

Only when the stories broke about how the office of the National Security Adviser, Ahmed Dasuki, had funded prayers for the re-election of President Jonathan did I realise that there was an entire political economy around prayers and elections, about which I had been clueless. According to one report, sometime before the 2015 elections, Sagir Bafawara, son of long time Nigerian political operative and former governor of Sokoto, Attahiru Bafawara, received over three billion naira from Ahmed Dasuki to procure marabouts from Saudi Arabia and parts of North Africa to pray for Jonathan.

Since Babangida moved into Aso Villa in 1991, few of the villa's occupants have not been associated with stories about prayers and marabouts in the context of remaining in power. The practice has become so pervasive that even a Christian like President Jonathan, who had knelt before Pastor Adeboye of the Redeemed Christian Church of God, would have no compunction in purchasing Muslim prayers. This is a country where the government and elite insist on reinforcing the importance of religion, interpreting all sorts of imagined slights on their religion or ethnicity to keep out merit and sustain divisions among an uneducated and impoverished population. There are hair-thin lines between the reliance on religion to divide and conquer; prayers for sale; the rise of super wealthy men of faith, and the occult practices that many politicians employ.

I remember thinking before the primaries that if prayers could win elections then surely my chances were good. But prayers – whether for free or for millions of dollars – are

no guarantee to winning elections in Nigeria. We were
probably not praying to the right god.

Chapter 11

Counting Down To P-Day

The primaries were two days away and still no one was quite sure what would happen. Would they take place at all? We, the outsiders and the aspirants who did not have approval from on high, got together at Hajiya Ireti's house to draw up a common position. We talked about what to expect at the meeting with the Department of State Security, to be held the next day, the eve of the big event. We wrote up recommendations and put them in a letter to the PDP chairman for the FCT, Y.Y. Sulaiman. We copied the letter to the FCT minister and Abubakar Mustapha, the PDP national organising secretary.

Our recommendations were:

1. The primaries should be conducted in a closed venue, to prevent thugs coming in. Veterans of past primaries felt the Old Parade Ground in Garki was too porous. The International Conference Centre would be more secure.

2. There should be no party designated writers for delegates. Delegates who were not literate and could not write should be allowed to choose who would write for them.

3. The delegates should carry proper identification, preferably their voters' cards.

4. The exercise should have one ballot box for all delegates. If the ballot boxes were separated between the two area councils, it would be easier to interfere with the votes of specific council delegates. It was widely known, for instance, that people of the Bwari and Abaji/Gwagwalada axis were unhappy with the incumbents and that the Bwari people were upset that one of their own had been prevented from contesting for the House.

5. We would need multiple tables, at least five, properly distanced from each other for delegates to write on.

6. After voting, delegates should be required to return to their seats, with no exceptions. The veterans told us that at contentious primaries, automatic delegates – the group that included incumbents and party leaders – would crowd round the ballot box and force the others to show them what they had written before casting their votes.

We also agreed amongst ourselves that we would walk out in protest if people moved sorted ballots from one pile to another, and if we noticed extra delegates at the venue.

It was early evening when Hajiya Ireti, Pastor Toyin Matthews, Kudambo, Esther and I, printed the letters and signed them. Esther was contesting for the other seat for the Abaji/Kuje/Kwali/Gwagwalada constituency. We travelled in two cars to the PDP Secretariat, where we were informed that we just missed Y.Y. The secretary and legal adviser were still in the office and received us in the conference room upstairs. We presented our issues and stated our case for the International Conference Centre instead of the Old Parade Ground. The Secretary suggested that cost was an issue. Still, he said they would do all they could to ensure security.

"If there is one thing I don't want, it is thuggery," the secretary said. "I am scared of it." An image flashed in my mind of a cat proclaiming a dislike for catching mice. I almost exploded from holding in my laughter.

In the final days of the race, the smell of upheaval was in the air. Pressure on delegates increased – there were meetings on what seemed like a daily basis with the incumbents, the party leadership and the FCT minister. From all accounts, it was a one-sided courtship. The delegates sat and received.

Gajo told me that at one meeting in a hotel in Apo, Hajiya Ireti indicated she had something to say, but could not catch the facilitator's attention no matter how hard she tried. Eventually she got up and, with her back to the high table, started addressing delegates about the need to protect their independence. The delegates cheered her wildly. It turned out that the delegates from the Abaji/Gwagwalada/Kuje/Kwali constituency refused to attend that meeting. They were not interested in instructions from above. The incumbent for that constituency, Dobi, ended up loosing the PDP primary election to his challenger, Danladi Zhin, who would in turn lose to the APC candidate in the general election.

It was just as well that I had not been made a delegate; at least I was spared these meetings. Instead, I could spend time on my campaign. I drafted daily text messages to all the delegates for Mayowa to send out. I continued to lobby ward-level party members and influencers. This led me to Olisa Uzoewulu. This was the person whom Charles, the City Centre delegate and engineer who received me at his home, had wanted me to contact.

Wulus, as he liked to be called, told me that I was unlikely to win. He himself had run for AMAC Area Council chairman in 1997, and lost. He had even written a book: *The Sad Event: The Struggle for the Abuja Municipal Area Council.*

"There is a small chance you might make it, but if you don't, it is not because you are not qualified," Wulus said. "It will be because of Nigeria's real godfather – political poverty. We think through our pockets, not through our brains. The Bwari people are bitter about how they have been treated, but will they translate their bitterness into action?"

"I have been transparent," I replied. "I have gone round, when other candidates have called the people to them. I know from the antecedents of the current legislators and what I have done and can do, that I am the better candidate. And even if I lose on Saturday, their conscience will prick them."

"No!" Wulus leapt forward on his seat, his legs vibrating urgently from the knees down. "Don't think that. The person with no work has no conscience. That is why people can't tell the truth about the bad things that people in office do."

He went on to tell us that he always knew Wowo's candidacy for Senate was not viable because of FCT politics. As someone who served at the pleasure of the FCT minister, he could not run for Senate without the minister's support and approval. And if the minister had instructions to deliver a particular person – even if he did not like or want that person – then this set his objectives on a collision course with establishment.

The stories were fascinating. It was hard to leave, but after almost an hour, we had to go. As we made our exit, Wulus threw out a final bit of advice.

"Pay close attention to the official delegate list when it is released," he said.

Hajiya Ireti, Esther and I arrived within minutes of each other for the meeting of aspirants with the DSS. It was held at the security service's FCT Command office in Asokoro. It was my first time in the place. The compound was huge, with the building in the middle, like a drop of stew on a tray of rice. The better to drown out screams I presumed. I was paranoid from tales of primaries laced with kidnappings and drugging. I had told my immediate family where I would be, and given them the mobile number from which I got the DSS invitation.

"If no one can reach me by 2p.m., please sound the alarm," I told them.

After half an hour, we moved from the director's office to a briefing room. The security team summarily proclaimed the security related rules for the primaries. Only aspirants contesting and their designated agents, delegates and officials conducting the primaries would be allowed into the venue. Any interlopers would be arrested.

The floor opened and Kudambo grabbed it.

He told the director that selective and secret meetings with delegates were taking place, and the actions of the party executives had created an unfair advantage for incumbents. There was a good chance that the delegate list, which had not been officially released twenty-four hours to the primaries, had been compromised.

Kudambo asked that in the interest of peace, all aspirants be accorded equal respect; otherwise some would be unable to control their supporters. According to him, the day before, Y.Y had disrespected him and had him manhandled when he entered his office while a meeting was taking place.

Soon, it was a free for all. The incumbents insisted at the top of their voices that in their dual capacity as aspirants and automatic delegates, they had a right to meet with the party chairman and the minister without other aspirants being invited. Non-incumbents complained that the party executives were ignoring their responsibilities, showing clear bias towards the government candidates, and ignoring the fact that if the primaries were simply free and fair, everyone would be happy and content with the results.

When I got a chance to speak, I pointed out that lack of information and transparency added to the tensions. The primaries were taking place the next day. Where was the venue? What time would the primaries start? How many agents could we bring?

The director said he was surprised that we did not have this information already.

Hajiya Ireti raised concerns about the security of the rumoured venue, the Old Parade Ground. The director admitted that the International Conference Centre was less porous and safer. But it was also a commercial space. Who would pay? Hajiya suggested that incumbents, being automatic delegates should pay. Everyone laughed.

The meeting wound up soon after. If nothing else, it provided the opportunity for aspirants to vent pent-up frustrations.

It was after Jumma'ah prayers, the afternoon before the primaries that I got notice that the official delegate list was finally out. City Centre had two delegates that I had never heard of. Charles was gone, and so was the female delegate. Gajo called to give me the news. He sent me the number for one of the new delegates. "Call her immediately," he shouted.

At that moment, Mayowa and I were on our way to GwaGwa's house. My lucky star was shining. GwaGwa had unexpected VIP guests, three automatic delegates whom I only knew by name and had not met until then. The names did not have any stories attached to them in terms of alliances.

I got a chance to tell them a little about myself. They were aware that I was in the race, and GwaGwa made it clear that I was his candidate. I could not give GwaGwa his delegate dues without giving them theirs, even though they were not in the budget. Still, I went home feeling smug.

That evening, as Mayowa and I prepared for the last meeting with the ad-hoc delegates later that night, Jamilu called. GwaGwa needed us to come see him immediately.

We learned that a meeting of delegates with the FCT minister had ended an hour or two before. They were told there was a presidency directive to return all the incumbents, and delegates would do well to follow orders. Threats and incentives were deployed. Some people spoke of fifty thousand naira, some of a hundred.

According to GwaGwa, after the minister finished his general tirade, flanked by the incumbents, he singled GwaGwa out for mention. They knew that he was not working for the party's candidates. When the meeting ended, the minister cornered GwaGwa and threatened his son's job.

In a voice I had to strain to hear, he told me he was not going to be able to vote for me. He wanted to let me know before I met with the delegates, so I could decide how to proceed. There was a brief silence.

I sat on the floor, in my usual position to the right of GwaGwa. I tried to pin down the thoughts swirling in my head. What did this mean? Was he withdrawing just his own vote, or were the votes of the delegates he controlled also gone? What had changed fundamentally? Was this the time to back out? Could I still back out? Did I want to back out?

Isiaka spoke first, asking me what I thought.

"Let us continue as planned," I said.

Jamilu and Isiaka exhaled.

I had not realised they were holding their breath. My words released the tension in the room. The atmosphere was moist from the steam escaping the human pressure cookers sitting around me. I thanked GwaGwa for the update. After all, one must never forget one's manners. Then we left.

As we got into the car, Mayowa noted that GwaGwa's disclosure was not accompanied by the return of the envelope I had given him less than six hours before.

Just before 11p.m., we drove into the Gombe Jewel Hotel, off Aminu Kano Crescent in Wuse 2, where we had reserved a suite. As we walked through the car park and lobby, we passed familiar faces. The delegates were waiting. We rode up the elevator and quickly reviewed our plans before receiving the delegates, grouped by ward, and their chairmen. Envelopes were ready: heavier for the delegates, lighter for the chairmen.

Jamilu had one last idea. People love humility; my frequent phone calls to delegates and chairmen to find out how they were doing and constant appeal for their support had apparently been effective. What we needed now was one final act of being the people's servant. Would I be averse to kneeling down as I give them their envelopes?

"Really?" I asked. "Would that make much of a difference?"

People like to be begged, Jamilu argued. That I could not disagree with. Nigeria's politics, like its roads, was littered with people begging, kneeling and prostrating their way into office or out of paying for their reckless driving.

Isiaka was sceptical, but I agreed to try it out.

Doing it for the first group was the hardest, but when I saw the reaction of the delegates and the chairman, it became easier. They were embarrassed and averted their eyes. They too begged. They said it was not necessary to beg them. They were with me. By the time we arrived at the Global Suites in Bwari, to repeat the exercise with the delegates, I was less vested in the routine. My knees had stopped co-operating, and the entire process felt seedy. I thought more than once about the symbolism of using hotels for these encounters. It was getting harder to differentiate the scammers from the *scammees* and the *screwers from the screwed.*

It was past 1a.m. when we left the hotel. Outside, the atmosphere was like being outside Moremi Hall at the University of Lagos on a Friday or Saturday night, when boys lined up their cars to shift girls to parties and clubs. The youth members were still up. Fatigue made it easy to ignore them.

As we got into the car, Jamilu suggested I leave some envelopes behind with him. We had agreed I would give every delegate their money by hand – no intermediaries. But the plan was to give dues to every Bwari delegate and we still had a few to cover. I left ten envelopes for Jamilu to distribute first thing in the morning.

When I got home, I waited up till I heard everyone was back to base. Then I went to bed. As I drifted off to sleep, I reviewed the flurry of last minute advice. I was not to pre-judge any person nor write anyone off. I had to give the delegates their due, without differentiating. Accept my enemy as my friend and remember that there were no permanent enemies in politics. It would serve me well to have a team of experts lined up for the primaries to spot irregularities and make sure my inexperience did not put me at a disadvantage.

Finally, and most important: I was not to turn my back on those who helped me get there.

Chapter 12

The Big Day

Primary election day had arrived! I woke up early to a deluge of text messages and missed calls. News of our overnight activities had spread far and wide, and missing delegates were coming out of the woodwork. One of them, Queen of Gwarimpa, was insistent. She would come to my house, she said, or she would wait for me at the junction or she could meet me at the venue gate. In the end, we met at the filling station opposite Transcorp Hilton. Queen came to the car with a man in tow. He too was a delegate; he would vote for me, they had discussed. I was relieved that I had extra envelopes. I handed them over. They were not in the plans or calculations, but that was a minor detail.

By 9.30a.m., we were at the party office in Garki. Except for office staff and a few automatic delegates, the office was deserted. The party flotsam had already moved to the Old Parade Ground, where the primaries were to be held. Still, no one could say what time it would start. I handed out envelopes to Josephine and the legal adviser who were on our list for AMAC and left for the Old Parade Ground.

In hindsight, I should have gone home, but I was too excited.

Outside the walls of the Old Parade Ground, a carnival of delegates, party officials, policemen, aspirants and hawkers milled around. Last minute negotiations, promises and threats were being traded along with pure water, drinks and recharge cards.

Hajiya Ireti was already there. She looked fabulous in ankara dress, Prada sunglasses and a small pouch slung across her body. I wore an Ankara dress as well, with pockets and soft black lace up shoes that would shield my feet from the dust. Pulling me aside, Hajiya Ireti tried to convince me to give something to the female delegate from Gui, as well as the two freshly minted delegates from City Centre and the woman leader for AMAC, Amina Haruna. I explained that we had done our analysis and Gui would not vote for me. Our analysis was simple: we were not bothering with the incumbents' wards, as there was no way I could win them.

I went to sit in the car to wait for the grounds to be opened. Mayowa joined me after a few minutes to work on me. We should listen to those who had been involved longer than we had, she told me. We had come this far – it would be a shame not to go all out at the end to ensure a win.

I had emergency cash, but was mindful that I had already given out more envelopes than we had intended. I had already been to the ATM and had reached my daily limit on all my cards.

I caved in and asked Mayowa to call the female Gui delegate and the woman leader. I was uneasy about the way the Gui woman could not meet my gaze, and I felt no guilt about giving her one of the lighter envelopes. As for Amina, she and I had built up a teasing rapport over the course of the campaign. She walked up to me pouting as she extended her hand to me. "*Haba, ba ki so ki yi da ni?*" she asked. So, you don't want to include me? I took her hand and led her to a quieter spot by the wall.

I told her I had heard that she and a few of the party executive committee members had received cars from one of the incumbents, and knew that her loyalties lay elsewhere.

She said it was not her fault if someone bought her a car. I reached into the huge multi-coloured cloth bag hanging from my shoulder and gave her one of the heavier envelopes. Her fingers closed around the envelope and she moved away. No thanks, no promise, not even a backward glance.

It was like that until the venue gates opened. I gave envelopes to another three delegates. One of them was the woman who gave Hajiya Zainab Maina attitude during the lunch with female delegates. Now, she walked up to me with an offer I could not refuse. "What do you mean by giving Josephine and Chinyere (legal adviser) money and leaving me out?" she said. "I will surely work against you inside." The other two were the City Centre delegates. The male delegate promised to send me a picture of my name on the ballot and took Mayowa's number. Around 11a.m., we finally streamed through the venue gates. I continued to hand out my cards to delegates to help them with spelling my name.

The space was staged carefully. The stands were for aspirants, their guests and family, the party notables and officials, the automatic delegates, incumbents, and policemen. On the field, there were tents and chairs set up for the ad-hoc delegates. They were a good hundred meters from the fence, and at least two hundred meters away from the stands. A security post was created in front of the entrance to the field, and marked with a red carpet. Armed men stood guard with instructions not to let anyone who was not a delegate or an official into the field. Jamilu joined the other agents for aspirants on a raised podium within the field. Abdulrahaman, one of my rivals for the AMAC/ Bwari ticket, had a problem securing an agent. While trying to sort that out, he walked back and forth audibly cursing. Some people in the stands jeered at him.

We were early, it seemed. I took a seat at the front row but moved around a bit, joining my sister Hadiza and Mayowa at the back a few times. We had brought coolers of drinks and snacks, and we shared them with the police and DSS around us. When security swept for people who were not supposed to be there, Mayowa and Hadiza remained invisible.

The automatic delegates started to fill up the stands. Everyone went round greeting and being greeted. Royalty like Alhassan GwaGwa sat while people flocked to them. After a round of greetings, I sat, watched, and engaged the people who landed next to me in this game of musical chairs. At one point, when Ngbako and I were sitting next to each other, a striking woman came to speak to him. She was tall, dark, colourfully dressed with an elaborate headgear. He introduced me to her, presenting me as one of the contestants.

She looked at me the way a lizard might look at an insect.

"Where are you from?" she asked

"FCT."

"Where in FCT?"

"Wuse Ward," I replied.

"Are you an indigene?"

"Who is an indigene?" I asked innocently.

She made a face and stepped away.

Later, I heard her talking loudly, pointedly within my earshot, about FCT people being wiser. But the music and my lack of interest made it hard to hear her.

By Zuhr prayers, a little past 1p.m., we were still sitting and waiting. There had been no announcements or sense of what we were waiting for. GwaGwa said he was tired and needed to pray. As I assisted him into his waiting jeep, he said he would not be back. Yusuf, his proxy, would cast his vote on his behalf.

Thirty minutes later, the FCT minister drove in right onto the red carpet. He came out, waved briskly towards the stands, and strode through the security barriers to talk with the delegates. A few people, including Aduda and Jisalo, went in after him. The minister moved from the AMAC tent to the Bwari tent; we could see him shaking hands and talking but could not hear what he had to say. Later, we were told that he reminded them of their previous discussions and their agreement to ensure the government candidates emerged victorious.

As soon as he left, the voting process began. It was clear that our request for a unified ballot box had been disregarded. By separating the ballot boxes, they would be able to tell where the majority of votes came from. This was how they could back up their threats.

The names of the delegates' were read out over the microphone. There were one hundred and eleven in total – two more than we should have had by my understanding. I had no idea who the extra two were; they were not on any list I had seen. In any case, even though I had seen many of the familiar delegates before the gates opened, I could not tell from the stands if the people in the field were in fact the same ones.

I rallied the other underdog contestants, Barrister Ushafa and Abdulrahaman, to get their agents to join Jamilu to raise a complaint and demand a single ballot box. But from the slow and deliberate way they reached for their phones, I could tell they did not care. We had a clear view of the agents on the podium, and I could see Jamilu talking to the officials. But the two ballot boxes stayed.

Strike one.

Next came the discussion about who would write for the delegates and who could not write. The announcer said that the chairman of the party for each area council would write for the delegates. Again, I tried to raise an alarm and insist that delegates should be free to ask anyone they want to write for them. Hajiya Ireti, being a delegate, was on the field. She called me to tell me to get my agent to protest. She had an interest in how the primaries for the House went, because it would set a precedent for the Senate primaries the next day. Despite best efforts and countless SMS messages to Jamilu, who was now answering the phone only when he felt like it, we could not get that instruction changed. "We should have spent lunch with the female delegates teaching them how to write my name," I said to Mayowa and Hadiza.

Strike two.

The incumbents, Aduda and Jisalo, and the other automatic delegates voted first. Most of the automatic delegates returned to the stands, but Aduda and Jisalo stayed behind. Through the fence, we could see that they had placed themselves at a vantage point right in front of the ballot boxes. Hajiya Ireti, who was still waiting to vote called me again and told me to get my agent to complain and get the other aspirants to complain as well. I started pestering Jamilu again. After several calls and text messages, he finally picked up. When I asked him to raise an objection, Jamilu told me the process was very fair. He spoke to me in the tone you would use to address the little boy who cried wolf too many times.

Strike three.

The results were announced. Jisalo had ninety-three votes; I had fourteen. Barrister Ushafa and Abdulrahaman had none. I had heard minutes earlier from Jamilu that Jisalo won. Still I was floored by the margin. Where did my fourteen votes come from? Jamilu said I had three from AMAC and eleven from Bwari.

I climbed down the stands to congratulate Jisalo and say better luck next time to the other contestants. Ambassador Ngbako came over to hug me and offer his congratulations for a gallant first attempt. A few of the automatic delegates, including one of the deacons I met in GwaGwa's house the day before, gave some words of encouragement. They made sure to add that there should be no bitterness.

Isiaka looked as if he had been crushed by a truck – crumpled, deflated, squinty, red-eyed and confused.

Jamilu was as perky as fresh picked mint. "We tried. *Haka Allah ya so,*" he said with a shrug. Then he walked away.

Chapter 13

Aftermath

After I lost the primaries, I could barely sleep for the first few nights. My mind kept spinning like the blades of a fan. When I did sleep, I saw the fourteen people who voted for me but as hard as I tried, I could not make out their faces. Who were they? Jisalo's ninety-three votes wore masks as well. My mind obsessed with pulling them off to see the ones I had eaten with and grown to like.

On the morning after the House primaries, my first call was to Hajiya Ireti. I had promised to accompany her to the Senate primaries, and called to find out when and where to meet.

"Ayisha! I have been calling you!" she said immediately.

"I turned off my phones," I said.

"I guessed as much."

"What is the plan for today? When are you going to Old Parade Ground?" I asked.

"Have you not heard? I have withdrawn from the race and left PDP. When I heard the results from yesterday, I could not believe it. The process is not transparent. I put out a press statement saying I was not participating and I have left the party."

It was the last thing I was expecting to hear.

I admitted I was shocked, not so much by Jisalo winning but by the margin. It was always a long shot. But where were all those angry Bwari votes? If Bwari was so intent on getting rid of Jisalo, how could I get only one-quarter of its delegates – eleven out of forty-four?

Hajiya Ireti disagreed with the tally. She said it was impossible that I got only three votes from AMAC. "Who told you that?" she demanded.

"Jamilu," I said.

"He is lying. If anything, it is the other way round. You got most of your votes from AMAC. AMAC has more people that cannot be bought or threatened."

I was in no position to argue.

"Go and get the papers," she said before the call ended. "You will see my statement."

"After close observation of the PDP FCT House of Representatives primary elections, conducted on December 6, 2014, I have come to the conclusion that the PDP FCT senatorial primaries will be neither free nor fair. Therefore, I am withdrawing from the PDP FCT senatorial race.

As the PDP has failed to offer a free, fair and democratic

platform, where all members can participate without fear or intimidation, I also withdraw from the membership of the party." – Ireti Kingibe, *Leadership*, 7 December 2014

Aduda took one hundred per cent of the votes in the Senate primaries. In the end, there was only Pastor Toyin Matthews to oppose him. Kudambo stepped down at the venue of the primaries but not before he delivered a long tortured speech about honouring the people who asked him to yield.

I stayed off the grid until Monday when Mayowa came to work to start winding up the campaign. Even then, the campaign phone stayed off and I turned off my personal phones for hours at a stretch.

Mayowa did not believe that the majority of my votes came from Bwari. She was convinced that Jamilu betrayed us. As we spoke to well-wishers over the following days, those from AMAC tried to convince me that most of my votes came from AMAC. Those from Bwari argued the opposite.

Unsolicited advice poured in about turning the loss to my benefit. "Take advantage of the situation and stay relevant," someone said. "Go and work on Jisalo's campaign or the president's; build on what you have achieved so far." Another suggestion was to make obeisance to the FCT party chairman. "Write Y.Y., thank him for his support, and offer yours." I declined to do any of these things.

Fortunately, that was not the tone when Isiaka, Jamilu and I went to see GwaGwa the following Tuesday. We focused on small talk about how the primaries went for both major parties. There were stories of delegates being beaten up by unsuccessful aspirants who wanted their money back. It was as if I had never been an aspirant. I listened, mostly. I realised through my sleep-deprived haze that I was there to make them feel better about themselves.

Closing down the campaign was not complicated. I did not owe anyone except Mayowa and a few printers. I settled all bills, sent text messages to the ward chairmen to thank them for their support and delivered milk, sugar and rice to the employees of the FCT PDP party office, in the spirit of Christmas and end of the year.

The visits were draining but cathartic. After the last one, I went home and slept until after midnight. I was jolted awake by a dream of Amina Haruna's gold-toothed smirk.

Epilogue

I was tired, but I wasn't traumatised. I had wanted the experience of contesting elections – a different kind of education – and I got it. Throughout the experience, the analytical side of my personality had been clicking along, observing the process, taking mental notes. Now, with the experience behind me, I began to write and think about what I had learned and what still left me puzzled.

I am confident that my choice of platform made no difference to the outcome, or to the lessons I learnt from the exercise.

What ails Nigerian political parties has taken years to develop. While our political parties have always taken on regional flavours, there was a stronger semblance of order and ideology in the past.

For instance, amongst the political parties active from 1979-1983, the values of the National Party of Nigeria were considered conservative; the Peoples Redemption Party was socialist, concerned with ending oppression and empowering the masses; and the United Party of Nigeria had similar welfarist ideals.

Anyone with knowledge about how political parties win elections in Nigeria would be unemotional about choosing between parties. With time, substantive differences between the parties have disappeared and today, the major parties, APC and PDP are quite similar. Amorphous parties, with no real difference in mode of operations, membership criteria, agenda or vision of society, will endure the same struggle to achieve meaningful results for the majority of citizens, and Nigerians will continue to engage with the same issues of poor service delivery and government dysfunction regardless of which party wins.

While our parties have always been works in progress, the parties of the Fourth Republic seem particularly repugnant in terms of how they are structured to operate. One theory about the state of our political parties today is that the decline started in November 1999, when Barnabas Gemade became PDP's first elected national chairman. Supported by President Obasanjo, who allegedly did not want the more independent minded Sunday Awoniyi, Gemade's emergence ushered in the era of the consensus candidate who served at the pleasure of whoever was president.

The First and Second Republic parties tried to maintain

discipline amongst members. President Shehu Shagari was known to attend meetings where Chief Adisa Akinloye, the NPN national chairman was in charge. Where elected officials refused to comply with party positions, there were usually costs – as was the case with Abubakar Rimi, one term governor of Kano, who, knowing he had alienated his PRP leadership, defected to NPP and lost his second term bid. Today, by force of precedence and deference, presidents and governors are considered leaders of their party and it is near impossible to hold them accountable.

Another turning point for PDP was the preparation for the 2007 elections when President Obasanjo, learning from his difficulties securing the PDP nomination for a second term, realised that he needed control over the party in order to determine his successor. This led to a process of de-registration and reregistration of PDP members across the country to flush out those who might assert themselves against his will. Soon, the governors mirrored the president as leaders at state level and none of them wanted members they could not control. One result of this system was that when governors started defecting from the PDP to the APC, they casually pushed aside the people who worked hard to establish APC in those states. Resentment from this leadership tussle continues to simmer in some states.

There are several levers that presidents and governors

use to exert their control over political parties. One is funding of the parties. Despite the substantial fees aspirants pay in order to contest the primaries, the parties have no discernable means of raising finance for their operations outside the election cycle. Membership dues are minimal, and the obligation stated in party rules that public officials pay a percentage of their basic salary to the party, like a tithe, is widely flouted. Instead, parties take the path of least resistance and raise funds by relying on governors, presidents, ex-governors, ex-presidents, a few other public officers and increasingly, some private sector operators. These are the people who have the disposable funds to invest in political parties and therefore dictate the tune in politics and government.

Another lever of control is the leadership structure of the party. The national and state working committees are not freely elected by party members, but filled by quasi enthronements, sometimes masked as elections. As a result, the leadership is rarely a team that works together in a shared commitment to build and strengthen the party. Instead, we have proxies whose main role is to serve factional and personal interests of their patrons.

A third lever of control is the delegate selection process and the operating manual for primaries. The fact that delegates are paid for their votes during party primaries is as secret as the location of a stock fish warehouse. But that isn't the complete picture either. Bottomless supplies of money for delegates still don't guarantee a primary election win. The support, endorsement, blessing or anointment of the party owners is required. While cash helps build and bind political relationships, there is typically a transactional history between the parties that is hard for new entrants or outsiders to overcome. Positions and promises are constantly traded within the political industry and around its edges – government contracts, jobs for children and placeholder positions as special assistants and teachers until the next elections. When all prospects for livelihood are tied to patrons in power, few can afford four years in political wilderness. When threatened with losing land rights or appointments, delegates will choose to play it safe.

There is another reason why delegates are not *the* sole key to winning primaries. According to court judgements such as Lado v. Congress for Progressive Change, the power to grant candidacy resides solely with a party's national working or executive committee. In other words, an aspirant might win the vote in a primary election, but the party on the national level might decide, for its own reasons, to submit a different person's name to the election management body as its candidate. The Supreme Court has declared that should such injustice take place, the person whose mandate was stolen has no recourse; the courts have no jurisdiction over the matter.

None of this reduces the need of aspirants to spend millions, even billions of naira to win office. It simply means the spending might not pay off. It begs the question: what are our political parties and political processes designed to deliver? Perhaps one day some mathematical model will show us the relationship between the state of Nigeria's development, our electoral process and the quality of candidates who win.

APC and PDP are currently caught in the throes of self-mutilation. Since the 2015 elections, neither party has been concerned with recruitment, rebranding, or financial innovation. For various reasons, neither of them has been able to hold party conventions to elect new leadership. Policy design and development is a distant dream.

The current president has a self-righteous disdain for the politicians he needed to become president. As such he does not consider himself the leader of the APC, or at least, has no interest in funding and controlling the party in the style of past presidents. This is not altogether a bad thing but there is a gap where alternative models should be. The tragedy is that while President Buhari could take advantage of the hunger for his approval to mold the party into something different from the norm, he has no eye on the future of politics and political parties in Nigeria. The leadership gap in the APC and the crisis in the PDP provide opportunities for others within and outside the parties to come up with strategies to develop real parties, not mere vehicles for winning elections. But the truth is that the existing model is easy and it explains why all parties operate the same way. The common operating model has produced stupendous individual results. As far as its owners and beneficiaries are concerned, it is not broken.

I am not convinced that the main obstacle to citizens demanding accountability and better services is a lack of information. Since 1960, in one form or another, the public has been inundated with facts and figures. Newspapers before the January 1966 coup were ripe with stories about mismanagement of public funds. Radio stations today keep track of all developments, giving the public the platform to air their views on the latest scandals. We knew at one point how much states and local governments got allocated from the federal budget every month. Any improvement to governance processes as a result of this information has been infinitesimal. Our political practices have not changed, and neither have our calculations around elections. Perhaps the problem is the quality of discussions around the information we have, which raises issues about education and exposure. There is an opportunity to translate what the information means to citizens (something which has begun) and organise more effectively around what should be done and why.

An example of the limits of information is that despite the clearly expressed unhappiness of the people of Bwari with their incumbent representative, for real and imagined slights, they still voted for a second term for Jisalo and could probably vote for him again.

Why?

Because in Nigeria our frames of reference are wrapped up in fear, identity, patronage, and social conditioning, and these veins run through the political elite and the general public alike.

Only quality education, in an environment of competitive human productivity and respect for law and justice, can cure this disease. No matter how good one's intentions, packaging information and delivering it to people who are similar to the dwellers in Plato's *Allegory of the Cave* is likely to be ill received. The information will be viewed with suspicion, and the motives of the messenger, questioned.

The problems with our political culture, electoral process, and lack of commitment to good governance on the part of elected officials are mutually compounding. A host of ills plague the country, for which there are accompanying excuses. We know some of what it will take to change the negative practices that accompany politics and elections in Nigeria and improve the legitimacy of our elections. Yet we are unwilling to make the necessary changes to the Constitution and our electoral laws and regulations. There are also small measures that the parties and the electoral commission could take on their own to improve transparency and legitimacy; but the people who benefit from current structures and processes have no incentive to change anything.

Those who think the political process is key to Nigeria's sustainable development have three choices: We continue to hope and pray that those who abuse their public positions will repent, convert to good governance and work on building sound institutions. We wait for a tipping point of public anger, which could bring violence and little actual advancement. Indeed, maybe something far worse than what we have today. We join the political parties and process in enough numbers that allows us to redesign our political parties, our elections, our government, and our country.

There is no doubt that we need more people participating as aspirants and candidates in the political space. The space is messy, but there is little choice but to continue to engage. What would make the difference is improving the structures and operations of the political parties to ensure transparent and accountable membership, self-financing, and fair, internal elections for the leadership of the parties. There would have to be accompanying modifications to our general election processes too, in order to complete the remodelling of our politics.

For those considering contesting elections, here are some survival tips:

Everyone can help you win, but it will cost you: You have to discern between the opportunists and the genuine, who will rarely come up to you to sell themselves. In politics people get paid on earth, not in heaven. Even when you live by this creed, there are no guarantees.

Make friends with the first ladies; get into their camp: Don't ask me how, but it can be done. They are useful to both male and female candidates – ask Wike. You may need to carry bags and sit on the floor. Keep your eye focused on the goal. You might not think you need them but then one day you might decide to run, and you'll be glad you invested in the relationship. Still, always remember: there are no guarantees.

Have your tax documents ready: If you think you might ever run for office, or may one day appear for a confirmation or screening hearing, have your tax clearance certificates up to date. Trying to get them during election season is a sign that you are a novice and it gives "them" leverage to gouge you.

Treasure your primary and secondary school leaving certificates: They are priceless, and by virtue of Sections 65(2)(a), 106(c), 131(d) and 177(d) of the Constitution, they are necessary to establish that you are eligible to run for office. If all else fails, be ready to swear an affidavit that your school leaving certificates were destroyed in a fire, stolen by your opponents or otherwise lost when you moved after completion of your doctorate degree.

Choose your campaign manager and agent carefully: You need someone you trust not to be swayed by bribes or intimidation, who will tell you when they've been approached, and who knows the tricks of the game. If the person thinks it's okay for the party chairman to fill in the ballot for the delegates who cannot write, this is not a good sign.

Do not assess your chances based on how much people claim your opponents are disliked or revile: Love is not a currency at the ballot.

Be deliberate about organising your campaign team: Resist the penchant for attributing titles, and do not rush to give out positions until you know the team better. Aim for a balance of political industry insiders and outsiders who represent all of your wards or constituencies, and truly understand the local characters and dynamics. Also, be careful who you let into the team regardless of how highly you hold the person who sent them. Sometimes you will have to accept team members even when you know they will be of no use. Be prepared to neutralise possible harm.

Mint banknotes are a must: The newer the notes, the greater the perception of your influence in the world. Have envelopes ready with fresh notes. Remember that smaller denominations make heavier envelopes. Colour-code or mark your envelopes so you know which ones hold five, ten or twenty thousand naira. This way, you can dole out money elegantly and efficiently – rather than prying notes out of rubber band restraints while navigating a crowd and pretending to hold a conversation.

Don't overthink it: You can't deal with all the temptations, crossroads and lines in the sand as hypotheticals. Instead, examine them when you face them. I wasted time vacillating between contesting and not contesting because of doubts and fears about what I would encounter, until I realised: *I will know it when I see it.* If nothing else, the experience will give you a truer sense of who you are.

The enemy of your enemy is not always your friend: The belief amongst my campaign team was that if the party leadership succeeded in coaxing Yohanna to drop out of the race, he would work against the party, or at least against Jisalo. When I talked to Yohanna before the primaries, he assured me of his support. Stopping just short of turning cartwheels after the results of the primaries were announced, no one seemed happier with the outcome than Yohanna.

You will spend more than you budgeted. Always.

Be prepared to practice being foolish: It's a valuable skill for life. Someone was lying to me; I knew and the person knew I knew. But we finished the required dance politely, and let everyone continue down their path.

Remember, the people know. I learned that the people in grassroots politics are not as unaware of social and political injustice as many well-intentioned outsiders believe. Visiting all the wards in my constituency, meeting local party officers, chairmen, and delegates, I found that people were clear and specific in their grievances. They were not happy about their current representation; they knew the reasons why they did not have roads or electricity. Yet, there is an enduring assumption among civil society organisations and donors that what people need most is information; that the more citizens know, the more they will demand. Something is missing.

Money is a lubricant: It eases open the doors of

influencers and party leaders. It is the microphone through which politicians are heard and understood. Without money, most aspirations would evaporate like steam. An idealistic focus on the corrupting nature of money in politics risks forgetting that contesting elections has real and legitimate costs.

Main Characters

What is a book about politics without a profile of main characters, even where some of the names have been changed?

Mallam Hassan

Fifty-years-old, portly Mallam Hassan is a smooth, seasoned talker with an encyclopaedic memory and the right answer for everything. An early bloomer within government, he is well connected and wealthy. How can one consult about their viability to contest if doors are not open? Mallam Hassan opens doors and who opens doors in politics is everything, in more ways than one.

Alhaji Liman

Well educated and reserved, Alhaji Liman at the end range of fifty years had served many presidents. He is one of the archetypal government children – those for whom, after a look at their résumé, one is tempted to exclaim, "Did they create the Nigerian government for you?"

Zephania Jisalo

Jisalo chaired Abuja Municipality Area Council (AMAC) from 2004 to 2010, and joined the House of Representatives in 2011 representing AMAC/Bwari constituency. Dark, stocky with a trademark, wide grin, he was the incumbent for the position I was contesting.

Ahmed Muazu

Tall and in his late fifties, Muazu's CV read like a yellow pages of Bauchi State public service. After serving as governor for two terms, he went national and was crowned the national chairman, People's Democratic Party in January 2014.

Al-Hassan GwaGwa

GwaGwa served as chairman of PDP for the Federal Capital Territory for twelve years, the longest anyone has served. Heavy, dark, and slow footed, GwaGwa looked to be in his late sixties, and was an automatic delegate for the primaries. He had battle scars from the 2011 primaries where his son lost to Jisalo in the contest for the AMAC/Bwari constituency ticket.

Amir

Lean and sprightly, Amir was instructed by Alhaji Liman to get me through certain doors. He introduced me to GwaGwa and the chairman of the PDP in the FCT, Y.Y. Sulaiman. After two visits together, his role was restricted

to being my lookout at Wadata Plaza for sightings of
Ahmed Muazu.

Hajiya Ireti Kingibe

I had heard about Hajiya Ireti long before I met her;
someone advised me to contact her as a valuable resource
on contesting elections. Tall, elegant and educated, Hajiya
Ireti was approachable and willing to share her experience
contesting elections with female politicians and civil society
organisations. Since 2003, she had made several attempts to
win a seat in the Senate and was intent on taking Senator
Philip Aduda's ticket away from him in 2015.

Zuby

I inherited Zuby, my first campaign team member from
Hajiya Ireti Kingibe's campaign operations. Small, dark and
wiry, Zuby was at least sixty, spoke little English and was a
seasoned operative of FCT's political industry.

Gajo

Gajo was chairman of the PDP in my ward, Wuse, and
critical to my emergence as an aspirant. Medium height and
in his thirties, he was a treasure hamper of PDP history
and political anecdotes.

Mayowa

The best personal assistant I did not know I could not live without. Mint note procurer, organiser extraordinaire and relationship smoother, this young, sleek lady, real life magician, thrived on impossible deadlines and project managing events.

Dr Ahmadu Ali

Dr Ali, almost eighty, had been in and around the Nigerian government and power holding blocs since the 1970s. As the former national chairman of PDP, he was still influential. His house was a Mecca for aspirants whom he regaled with anecdotes of elections he had contested and governors he had crowned.

Peter Yohanna

Yohanna, dark skinned and boisterous, looked like he was in his early to mid-thirties (accounting for the "small boy" moniker). The PDP establishment considered him the most serious challenger to Jisalo's incumbency at the House of Representatives.

Isiaka

Isiaka, educated, respectable and soft spoken, was in his thirties. He was part of Bwari PDP establishment by virtue of his advisory position to Peter Yohanna, the chairman of Bwari Area Council. He was one of my key campaign advisers.

Jamilu

Jamilu was a clone of Isiaka. He was the same age, educated, young family man and part of the Bwari PDP family albeit as a stepchild by virtue of the position of his principal, Matawalle, the deputy chairman of Bwari Area Council. Jamilu was introduced as a possible manager for the Bwari campaign and ended up as my agent on the day of the primaries.

What I Told The President

November 12 2014

Dr. Goodluck Ebele Jonathan GCFR, GCON

President, Federal Republic of Nigeria

Aso Rock Villa

Three Arms Zone

Abuja

Dear Mr. President,

I must start with full disclosure. I am an aspirant vying for the Peoples Democratic Party's ticket to represent the AMAC/ Bwari Constituency in the House of Representatives in 2015. I write only on the premise of a saying in Hausa "ba mugun sarki, sai mugun waziri" (there are no wicked kings, only wicked advisers). Many in Nigeria would like to believe this. It would, quite simply, explain a lot.

In the Federal Capital Territory, great home to the Federal Government, the scene is being set to prepare members of our party for the possibility of automatic endorsements for the current legislators. Sir, this would be a grave mistake because if primaries do not hold in the FCT, it could very likely result in the PDP losing the general elections for the national assembly.

People are wondering, who is advising the President? We ask because the plans that are being proposed are not in the best interest of Nigerians, democracy and the maturity and stability of the PDP. If you, and by extension the rest of us, are not at the mercy of wicked advisers, this is some of what you would hear regarding the primaries and the importance of precedents in our democracy.

First, giving the PDP Governors carte blanche to choose their successors undermines our democracy. Governors are not monarchs and there is nothing in our legal framework to support this. People should be able to choose who should govern them and politicians have a right to a level playing field within which to compete to serve their people as governors. Besides, since 2007, not one of the previous governors who determined their successors has had the type of control they assumed they would have. Not Attah. Not Obi. Not even Tinubu.

Second, despite the persuasive arguments in favour of continuity for legislators in order to build expertise within the national and state assemblies, this should not be at the expense of developing our democracy and building the trust that citizens should have in the electoral process. If a legislator has served to the satisfaction of the constituency, then that constituency should be the determining factor. Securing the party's nomination to contest should not be automatic for incumbents.

Third, the domino effect of automatic tickets for incumbent governors, senators, representatives etc. is that party members who have been planning for the elections, for years will be left high and dry. Years of constituency engagements wasted. Many are likely to decamp to other parties, taking their structures with them and working against the interest of the PDP.

Fourth, Mr. President, voter apathy is real. Any straw poll even in the heart of the Federal Capital Territory will tell you how disengaged people are with the electoral process. Some have completely given up that meaningful change will happen through the ballot and part of the reason is the over familiar faces of the contestants across all the parties. If status quo, automatic tickets and consensus (in favour of incumbent) are the reigning philosophies for the PDP primaries, how are new entrants going to come in? The Republicans just won by a landslide in the US mid-term elections. The votes were not just a reaction to President Obama's policies. The Republicans deliberately embraced the demographics of the nation and acceded to the human desire for inclusion. For the first time in history some States voted in African Americans on the Republican ticket and the youngest ever woman voted into Congress at thirty years, was fielded by the Republican party. Can PDP take a deliberate decision to ensure more women, young people and disabled people get increased representation in 2015?

Finally, Mr. President, blackmail is not acceptable. If the distinguished elders of our party decided in their wisdom to give you their full endorsement and the right of first refusal to be the Presidential flag bearer, then they should not be allowed to turn round and insist on the same privileges. The Presidency is special – but no to automatic tickets for Senators and others, that is not how democracy is designed. Do not endorse an extremely bad precedent from which we might not recover.

Beyond roads, bridges, trains and airports, your legacy must include the nurturing and strengthening of our democracy. Please do not be the President who injected steroids to the stranglehold which the Governors and some legislators have on our collective throats. Let democracy breathe and thrive.

I beg your pardon Mr. President but if there is no response to this letter within ten days from the date of this letter, I will publish it in as many news and media outlets as possible. This is because with no assurance that your advisers would have brought my letter to your attention, it will be my only other medium for sharing my views with you.

Sincerely,
Ayisha Osori

Cc.

Governor Ahmed Muazu,

National Chairman, People's Democratic Party

Y.Y. Sulaiman,

FCT Chairman, People's Democratic Party

Ayisha is a lawyer and consultant with over eighteen years experience in the public and private sectors including working with the World Bank, United Nations Children's Fund, and Department of International Development on projects related to good governance, gender equality, women's economic and political participation and ending violence against women.

She is a published writer with a series of children's text books on social studies used in primary schools and a children's reference book on Nigeria. She kept a weekly column for five years, in *Thisday's The Lawyer* newspaper and most recently, as the *Nigerian Citizen* for the *Leadership* newspaper where she covered legal and social issues ranging from state sponsored marriages to good governance. Ms. Osori is a regular commentator on radio and television and has been involved in numerous campaigns to improve social justice for women and girls and to improve governance in Nigeria.

Ms. Osori, an Eisenhower Fellow, graduated from the University of Lagos and Harvard Law School with degrees in law and has a Masters in Public Administration from the Harvard Kennedy School. She is licensed to practice law in Nigeria and the State of New York.